MARTIN PISTORIUS was born in Johannesburg, South Africa, in 1975. An unknown illness at the age of twelve left him wheelchair-bound and unable to speak, and he spent fourteen years in institutions. In 2001 he learned to communicate via computer, make friends and change his life. In 2008 he met the love of his life, Joanna, and emigrated to the UK. In 2009 they married and in 2010 he started his own business. He describes himself as a geek with a wicked sense of humour and a love of technology. He loves animals, is a keen photographer, enjoys watching cricket, Formula 1 Grand Prix and films, listening to music, spending time with friends and, most of all, being with his wife.

Praise for *Ghost Boy*

'It is a deeply affecting and at times shocking book . . . *The Diving-Bell and the Butterfly* but with a happy ending' *Sunday Times*

'Deeply moving' *Mail on Sunday*

'Deeply affecting memoir' *Sunday Times Best Reads*

'[Pistorius's] levels of empathy are remarkable, perhaps because he was forced for so many years into the role of watcher and listener, hearing people unburden their problems around him, absorbing their pain without them knowing . . . [his] communication is strikingly direct, almost fearless in the way he confronts emotional reality' *Scotland on Sunday*

Ghost Boy

Martin Pistorius

and

Megan Lloyd Davies

**SIMON &
SCHUSTER**

London · New York · Sydney · Toronto · New Delhi

First published in Great Britain by Simon & Schuster UK Ltd, 2011
This edition published in Great Britain by Simon & Schuster UK Ltd, 2012

7 9 10 8 6

Simon & Schuster UK Ltd
1st Floor
222 Gray's Inn Road
London WC1X 8HB

www.simonandschuster.co.uk

Simon & Schuster Australia, Sydney
Simon & Schuster India, New Delhi

A CIP catalogue record for this book
is available from the British Library.

ISBN: 978-1-47115-100-2
ISBN: 978-0-85720-332-8 (ebook)

Typeset by M Rules
Printed and bound by CPI Group (UK) Ltd, Croydon CR0 4YY

MIX
Paper | Supporting
responsible forestry
FSC
www.fsc.org   FSC® C171272

For my wife, Joanna,
who listens to the whispers of my soul
and loves me for who I am

Contents

Prologue

Barney the Dinosaur is on the TV again. I hate Barney — and his theme tune. It's sung to the notes of 'Yankee Doodle Dandy'.

I watch children hop, skip and jump into the huge purple dinosaur's open arms before looking at the room around me. The children here lie motionless on the floor or slumped in seats. A strap holds me upright in my wheelchair. My body, like theirs, is a prison that I can't escape: when I try to speak, I'm silent; when I will my arm to move, it stays still.

There is just one difference between me and these children: my mind leaps and swoops, turns cartwheels and somersaults as it tries to break free of its confines, conjuring a lightning flash of glorious colour in a world of grey. But no one knows because I can't tell them. They think I'm an empty shell, which is why I've been sitting here listening to *Barney* or *The Lion King* day in, day out, for the past nine years, and just when I thought it couldn't get any worse, *Teletubbies* came along.

I'm twenty-five years old but my memories of the past only begin from the moment I started to come back to life from wherever I'd been lost. It was like seeing flashes of light in the darkness as I heard people talking about my sixteenth birthday and wondering whether to shave the stubble on my chin. It scared me to listen to what was being said because, although I had no memories or sense of a past, I was sure I was a child and the voices were speaking about a soon-to-be man. Then I slowly realised it was me they were discussing, even as I began to understand that I had a mother and father, brother and sister I saw at the end of every day.

Have you ever seen one of those movies in which someone wakes up as a ghost but they don't know they've died? That's how it was, as I realised people were looking through and around me and I didn't understand why. However much I tried to beg and plead, shout and scream, I couldn't make them notice me. My mind was trapped inside a useless body, my arms and legs weren't mine to control and my voice was mute. I couldn't make a sign or a sound to let anyone know I'd become aware again. I was invisible – the ghost boy.

So I learned to carry my secret and became a silent witness to the world around me as my life passed by in a succession of identical days. Nine years have passed since I became aware once more and during that time I've escaped using the only thing I have – my mind – and to explore everything from the black abyss of despair to the psychedelic landscape of fantasy.

That's how things were until I met Virna, and now she alone suspects there's an active consciousness hidden inside me. Virna believes I understand more than anyone thinks possible. She wants me to prove it tomorrow when I'm tested at a clinic specialising in giving the silent a voice, helping everyone – from those with Down's syndrome and autism to brain tumours or stroke damage – to communicate.

Part of me dares not believe this meeting might unlock the person inside the shell. It took so long to accept I was trapped inside my body – to come to terms with the unimaginable – that I'm afraid to think I might be able to change my fate. But, however fearful I am, when I think about the possibility that someone might finally realise I'm here, I can feel the wings of a bird called hope beating softly inside my chest.

Counting Time

I spend each day in a care home in the suburbs of a large South African city. Just a few hours away are hills covered in yellow scrub where lions roam looking for a kill. In their wake come hyenas that scavenge for leftovers and finally there are vultures hoping to peck the last shreds of flesh off the bones. Nothing is wasted. The animal kingdom is a perfect cycle of life and death, as endless as time itself.

I've come to understand the infinity of time so well that I've learned to lose myself in it. Days, if not weeks, can go by as I close myself down and become entirely black within – a nothingness that is washed and fed, lifted from wheelchair to bed – or I immerse myself in the tiny specks of life I see around me. Ants crawling on the floor exist in a world of wars and skirmishes, battles being fought and lost, with me the only witness to a history as bloody and terrible as that of any people.

I've learned to master time instead of being its passive

recipient. I rarely see a clock but I've taught myself to tell the time from the way sunlight and shadows fall around me after realising I could memorise where the light fell whenever I heard someone ask the time. Then I used the fixed points that my days here give me so unrelentingly – morning drink at 10 a.m., lunch at 11.30, an afternoon drink at 3 p.m. – to perfect the technique. I've had plenty of opportunity to practise, after all.

It means that now I can face the days, look at them square on and count them down minute by minute, hour by hour, as I let the silent sounds of the numbers fill me – the soft sinuousness of sixes and sevens, the satisfying staccato of eights and ones. After losing a whole week like this, I give thanks that I live somewhere sunny. I might never have learned to conquer the clock if I'd been born in Iceland. Instead I'd have had to let time wash over me endlessly, eroding me bit by bit like a pebble on the beach.

How I know the things I do – that Iceland is a country of extreme darkness and light or that after lions come hyenas, then vultures – is a mystery to me. Apart from the information that I drink in whenever the TV or radio is switched on – the voices like a rainbow path to the pot of gold that is the world outside – I'm given no lessons nor am I read to from books. It makes me wonder if the things I know are what I learned before I fell ill. Sickness might have raddled my body but it only took temporary hostage of my mind.

It's midday now, which means there are less than five hours to go before my father comes to collect me. It's the brightest moment of any day because it means the care home can be left behind at last when Dad picks me up at 5 p.m. I can't describe how excited I feel on the days my mother arrives after she finishes work at 2.

I will start counting now – seconds, then minutes, then hours – and hopefully it will make my father arrive a little quicker.

One, two, three, four, five . . .

I hope Dad will turn on the radio in the car so that we can listen to the cricket together on the way home.

'Howzat?' he'll sometimes cry when a ball has been bowled.

It's the same if my brother David plays computer games when I'm in the room.

'I'm going up to the next level!' he'll occasionally shriek as his fingers fly across the console.

Neither of them has any idea just how much I cherish these moments. As my father cheers when a six is hit or my brother's brow knits in frustration as he tries to better his score, I silently imagine the jokes I would tell, the curses I would cry with them, if only I could, and for a few precious moments I don't feel like a bystander any more.

I wish Dad would come.

Thirty-three, thirty-four, thirty-five . . .

My body feels heavy today and the strap holding me up cuts through my clothes into my skin. My right hip aches. I wish someone would lie me down and relieve the pain. Sitting still for hours on end isn't nearly as restful as you might imagine. You know those cartoons when someone falls off a cliff, hits the ground and smashes – kerpow! – into pieces? That's how I feel – as if I've been shattered into a million pieces and each one is hurting. Gravity is painful when it's bearing down on a body that's not fit for the purpose.

Fifty-seven, fifty-eight, fifty-nine. One minute.

Four hours, fifty-nine minutes to go.

One, two, three, four, five . . .

Try as I might, my mind keeps returning to the pain in my hip. I think of the broken cartoon man. Sometimes I wish I could hit the ground as he does and be smashed into smithereens. Because maybe then, just like him, I could jump up and miraculously become whole again before starting to run.

2

The Deep

Until the age of twelve, I was a normal little boy – shyer than most maybe and not the rough-and-tumble kind but happy and healthy. What I loved most of all was electronics and I had such a natural ability with them that my mother trusted me to fix a plug socket when I was eleven because I'd been making electronic circuits for years. My flair also meant I could build a reset button into my parents' computer and rig up an alarm system to protect my bedroom from my younger brother and sister, David and Kim. Both were determined to invade my tiny Lego-filled kingdom but the only living thing allowed to enter it, apart from my parents, was our small yellow dog called Pookie, who followed me everywhere.

Over the years I've listened well during countless meetings and appointments, so I learned that in January 1988 I came home from school complaining of a sore throat and never went back to classes again. In the weeks and months that followed, I stopped eating, started sleeping for hours every day and complained of how painful it was to walk. My body began to weaken as I stopped using it and so did my mind: first I forgot facts, then familiar things like watering my bonsai tree and finally even faces.

To try and help me remember, my parents gave me a frame of family photos to carry around, and my mother, Joan, played me a video of my father, Rodney, every day when he went away on business. But while they hoped the repetition might stop the memories slipping from my mind, it didn't work. My speech deteriorated as I slowly forgot who and where I was. The last words I ever spoke were about a year after I first got ill as I lay in a hospital bed.

'When home?' I asked my mother.

But nothing could reach me as my muscles wasted, my limbs became spastic and my hands and feet curled in on themselves like claws. To make sure I didn't starve as my weight plummeted, my parents woke me up to feed me. As my father held me upright, my mother spooned food into my mouth and I swallowed instinctively. Other than that, I didn't move. I was completely unresponsive. I was in a kind of waking coma that no one understood because the doctors couldn't diagnose what had caused it.

At first, the medics thought my problems were psychological and I spent several weeks in a psychiatric unit. It was only when I was taken to casualty suffering from dehydration after the psychologists failed to persuade me to eat or drink that they finally accepted my illness was physical and not mental. So brain scans and EEGs, MRI scans and blood tests were done, and I was treated for tuberculosis and cryptococcal meningitis but no conclusive diagnosis was made. Medication after medication was tried – magnesium chloride and potassium, amphotericin and ampicillin – but to no effect. I'd travelled beyond the realms of what medicine understood. I was lost in the land where dragons lie and no one could rescue me.

All my parents could do was watch me slip away from them day by day: they tried to keep me walking but I had to be held up as my legs got weaker and weaker; they took me to hospitals all over South Africa as test after test was run but nothing was found; and they wrote desperate letters to experts in America, Canada and England, who said their South African colleagues were surely doing all that could be done.

It took about a year for the doctors to confess that they had run out of treatment options. All they could say was that I was suffering from a degenerative neurological disorder, cause and prognosis unknown, and advise my parents to put me into an institution to let my illness run its course. Politely but firmly the medical profession washed its hands of me as my mother and father effectively were told to wait until my death released us all.

So I was taken home, where I was cared for by my mother, who gave up her job as a radiographer to look after me. Meanwhile my father worked such long hours as a mechanical engineer that he often didn't get home to see David and Kim before they went to bed. The situation was untenable. After about a year at home, at the age of fourteen it was decided that I should spend my days in the care centre where I am now but I'd go home each night.

Years passed with me lost in my dark, unseeing world. My parents even tried putting mattresses on the living-room floor so that they, Kim and David could all live as I did – at floor level – in the hope of reaching me. But I lay like an empty shell, unaware of anything around me. Then, one day, I started coming back to life.

Last 'normal' family photo taken in 1987

3

Coming Up for Air

I'm a sea creature crawling along the ocean floor. It's dark here. Cold. There's nothing but blackness above, below and all around me.

But then I begin to see snatches of light glimmering overhead. I don't understand what they are.

Something tells me I must try to reach them. It drives me upwards as I kick towards the shards of light, which skitter across the surface far above me. They dance as they weave patterns of gold and shadow.

*

My eyes focus. I'm staring at a skirting board. I'm sure it looks different than it normally does but I don't know how I know this.

*

A whisper across my face – wind.

*

I can smell sunshine.

*

Music, high and tinny. Children singing. Their voices fade in and out, loud then muffled, until they fall silent.

*

A carpet swims into view. It's a swirl of black, white and brown. I stare at it, trying to make my eyes focus but the darkness comes for me again.

*

A wash cloth is pushed cold across my face and I feel my cheek flame in disapproval as a hand holds my neck steady.

'I won't take a second,' a voice says. 'We've got to make sure you're a clean boy now, haven't we?'

*

The snatches of light become brighter. I'm getting closer to the surface. I want to break through it but I can't. Everything is too fast whereas I am still.

*

I smell something.

I drag my eyeballs upwards. They feel so heavy.

A little girl is standing in front of me. She is naked from the waist down. Her hand is smeared brown. She giggles as she tries to open the door.

'Where are you going, Miss Mary?' a voice asks as a pair of legs appears at the edge of my vision.

I hear the door being closed and then a grunt of disgust.

'Not again, Mary!' the voice exclaims. 'Look at my hand!'

The little girl laughs. Her delight is like a ripple of wind carving a groove in sand running smooth across a deserted beach. I can feel it vibrating inside me.

*

A voice. Someone is speaking. Two words: sixteen and death. I don't know what they mean.

*

It's night-time. I'm in my bed. Home. I gaze around in the half-darkness. A row of teddy bears lies beside me and there's something on my feet. Pookie.

But as the familiar weight disappears, I can feel myself rising. I'm confused. I'm not in the sea. I'm in real life now. But still I feel as if I'm floating, leaving my body and moving upwards towards my bedroom ceiling.

Suddenly I know that I'm not alone. Reassuring presences are wrapping themselves around me. They comfort me. They want me to follow them. I understand now that there's no reason to stay here. I'm tired of trying to reach the surface. I want to let go, give myself up to the deep or to the presences that are with me now – whichever takes me first.

But then one thought fills me: I can't leave my family.

They are sad because of me. Their grief is like a shroud that envelops me whenever I break through the surface of the waves. They'll have nothing to grab on to if I leave. I can't go.

Breath rushes into my lungs. I open my eyes. I'm alone again. Whatever was with me is gone.

Angels.

I have decided to stay.

4

The Box

Even as I became aware, I didn't fully understand what had happened to me. Just as a baby isn't born knowing it can't control its movements or speak, I didn't think about what I could or couldn't do. Thoughts rushed through my mind that I never considered voicing and I didn't realise the body I saw jerking or motionless around me was mine. It took time for me to understand I was completely alone in the middle of a sea of people.

But as my awareness and memories slowly started to mesh together and my mind gradually reconnected to my body, I began to understand I was different. Lying on the sofa as my father watched gymnastics on TV, I was fascinated by the bodies that moved so effortlessly, the strength and power they revealed in every twist and turn. Then I looked down at a pair of feet I often saw and realised they belonged to me. It was the same with the two hands that trembled uncontrollably whenever I saw them nearby. They were part of me too but I couldn't control them at all.

I wasn't paralysed: my body moved but it did so independently of me. My limbs had become spastic. They felt distant, as if they were encased in concrete, and I couldn't control them. People were always trying to make me use my legs – physios bent them in painful contortions as they tried to keep the muscles working – but I couldn't move unaided.

If I ever walked, it was to take just a few shuffling steps with someone holding me up because otherwise I would crumple to the floor. If I tried to feed myself, my hand would smear food across my cheek. My arms wouldn't instinctively reach out to protect me if I fell so I'd hit the ground face first. I couldn't roll myself over if I was lying in bed so I'd stay in the same position for hours on end unless someone turned me. My limbs didn't want to open up and be fluid; instead they curled into themselves like snails disappearing into shells.

Just as a photographer carefully adjusts his camera lens until the picture becomes clear, it took time for my mind to focus. But while my body and I were locked in an endless fight, my mind was slowly getting stronger as the pieces of my consciousness knitted themselves together.

Gradually I became aware of each day and every hour in it. Most were forgettable but there were times when I watched history unfold. Nelson Mandela being sworn in as president in 1994 is a hazy memory while Diana's death in 1997 is clear.

I think my mind started to awaken at about the age of sixteen and by nineteen it was fully intact once more: I knew who I was and where I was, and I understood that I'd been robbed of a real life. I was completely entombed.

That was six years ago. At first I wanted to fight my fate by leaving some tiny sign to guide people back to me, like the pieces of bread Hansel and Gretel left behind to help them find their way out of the dark woods. But gradually I came to understand that my efforts would never be enough: even as I came back to life, no one fully understood what was happening.

As I slowly regained enough control of my neck to start jerking my head down and to the right, lifting it occasionally or smiling, people didn't realise what my new movements meant. They didn't believe miracles happened twice: I'd already survived doctors' predictions that I would surely die so no one thought to look for divine intervention a second time. As I started 'replying' yes or no to simple questions with a turn of my head or a smile, they thought it showed only the most basic improvement. No one considered that my improved responses might mean my intelligence was some-how intact. They'd been told long ago that I was severely brain-damaged so when the young man with stick-like limbs, empty eyes and drool running down his chin occasionally lifted his head that's what they saw.

And so I was cared for – fed and watered, wiped and cleaned – but never really noticed. Again and again I'd ask my unruly limbs to make a sign and show someone I was still there but they would never do as I asked.

I'm sitting on my bed. My heart is beating as my father undresses me. I want him to know, to understand that I've returned to him. He must see me!

I stare at my arm, willing it to work. Every bit of me condenses into this moment. I stare at my arm – pleading, cajoling, admonishing and begging. My heart leaps as I feel it respond to my pleas. My arm is waving high above my head. At last I'm leading the way back to myself with the kind of sign I've spent so long trying to make.

But when I look at my father, neither shock nor surprise is written on his face. He simply carries on pulling off my shoes.

Dad! I'm here! Can't you see?

But my father doesn't notice me. He continues to undress me and my gaze slides unwillingly to my arm. It's only then I realise it's not moving. However powerful my hope seems, its only outward manifestation is a muscular twitch close to my elbow. The movement is so tiny I know my father will never notice it.

Rage fills me. I feel sure I'll burst. I gasp for breath.

'Are you okay, boy?' Dad asks as he hears my ragged breathing and looks up.

I can do nothing but stare at him, praying that my silent desperation will somehow communicate itself.

'Let's get you into bed, shall we?'

A pyjama top is pulled on over my head and I'm laid down. Anger bites into my stomach. I know I must switch it off: it will hurt too much if I don't. I must lose myself in nothingness or else I'll go mad.

At other times I tried to groan, hoping that if a noise escaped my chest someone would wonder what it meant, but I could never make a sound. In later years I'd sometimes try to speak but I was always silent. I couldn't pick up a pen to scrawl a message or utter a plea for help. I was marooned on the island of myself, and hope guttered inside me as I realised that I would never be rescued.

Horror came first, then bitter disappointment, and I turned in on myself to survive. Like a turtle retreating into its shell, I learned to escape reality in fantasy. I knew I was going to spend the rest of my life as powerlessly as I lived each present day and eventually I didn't try to respond or react but stared at the world with a blank expression.

To other people, I resembled a pot plant: something to be given water and left in the corner. Everyone was so used to me not being there that they didn't notice when I began to be present again.

I'd been put into a box long before, after all. Each of us has. Are you the 'difficult' child or the 'histrionic' lover, the 'argumentative' sibling or the 'long-suffering' spouse? Boxes make us easier to understand but they also imprison us because people don't see past them.

We all have fixed ideas of each other even though the truth can be far removed from what we think we see. That is why no one asked what it might mean when I started to improve enough to answer simple questions like 'Would you like tea?' with a turn of my head or a smile.

For most of the people who met me, I was just a job. To the staff at my care home, I was a familiar fixture they didn't take any notice of after so many years; to care workers at other places I was sent when my parents went away, I was just a passing patient; and for the doctors who saw me, I was 'the one who can't do too much', as one memorably told his colleague while I lay like a starfish on an X-ray table.

Meanwhile, my parents had full-time jobs and two other children to look after as well as me but they did everything from changing my nappy to cutting my toenails. Attending to my physical needs took so much time and energy, it's no surprise my mother and father didn't stop to think about whether I'd defied medical odds and had a recovery that was nothing short of a miracle.

So that's why I stayed inside the box I'd been put into so long before. It was the one marked with a single word: 'imbecile'.

Dad (Rodney) and Martin sitting on the couch at home

5

Virna

The smell of the mandarin oil is sharp but sweet as Virna massages my arm. Her hands move seamlessly as she works the leaden muscles. As I stare at her, she raises her head to smile at me and I wonder yet again why I didn't notice hope when it first arrived in my life.

To begin with, all I knew was that Virna never showed her teeth when she smiled and she twitched her leg nervously as she sat cross-legged in a chair. She'd started working at my care home as a relief carer and I noticed such details about her because that's what you learn to do when people don't talk to you. But then Virna started speaking to me and I realised she was someone I could never forget. Most people speak at, around, over or about me so anyone who treats me like a cut above the average root vegetable is unforgettable.

One afternoon Virna told me her stomach was aching. It's the kind of everyday confession I've heard for years as people have chatted unguardedly, thinking I'm not really with them. What I don't know about some of the carers' health problems is hardly worth knowing: one has a husband with Alzheimer's, another has problems with her kidneys and one woman's vaginal tumour almost left her childless.

But when Virna spoke to me it was different. She wasn't talking to herself, someone else or even the empty room like most people do. She was speaking to me, chatting as she would to anyone her own age about the thoughts that floated through her mind like dust motes in sunlight. It was a conversation any twenty-something friends might have but I'd never experienced it before. Soon Virna started telling me about everything from the sadness of her grandmother's illness to the new puppy she'd got and the boy she was excited to be going on a date with. I felt almost as if I was making my first friend.

That was the reason I started looking at Virna, which is not something I often do. My head usually feels like a breeze block when I try to lift it and I'm rarely at the same eye level as other people because I'm always sitting in a chair or lying down. It takes so much effort that a long time ago I gave up making eye contact with people who look but never see. I sit for hours each day staring blankly into space. But that changed when Virna began giving me and some of my fellow inmates aromatherapy massages to soothe our twisted limbs. Lying on my back while she kneaded my aching muscles, I was able to let my eyes follow her as she spoke to me and bit by bit I started to peep out from the shell I'd retreated into.

Virna looked at me properly, which was something no one

had done for a long time. She saw that my eyes really were the windows to my soul and became more and more convinced that I understood what she said. But how could she convince anyone else that the unresponsive ghost boy was capable of more?

Months turned into one year and then two. Then about six months ago Virna saw a TV programme about a woman who'd been helped to communicate after being rendered mute by a stroke. Soon afterwards Virna went to an open day at a nearby centre where she'd heard experts talk about what could be done to help those who can't speak and she came back excited to tell me about what she'd learned.

'They use switches and electronic devices to help people communicate,' she said. 'Do you think you could do something like that, Martin? I'm sure you could.'

Other care staff had also gone to the open day but weren't as convinced as Virna was that I might be a suitable candidate.

'Do you really think he's got it in him?' one of them asked.

The woman bent towards me with the shadow of a grin on her face and I smiled to try and show her that I understood what she was saying. But my only two gestures – jerking my head down to the right and smiling – are interpreted as the knee-jerk reactions of an undeveloped mind, the kind of responses that any six-month-old baby can make, so she didn't take any notice.

The carer looked at me and sighed as her grin faded. I wondered if she knew that her breath was bitter from the coffee she'd recently been drinking.

'Can you imagine anything so ridiculous?' she said later to

her friend after Virna had left. 'There's no way any of them could communicate.'

The two women looked around the room.

'Maybe Gertje?'

They looked at a little boy who was playing with a toy car nearby.

'He's a bit better than some, isn't he?'

The women were silent for a moment before their eyes came to rest on me. They didn't say anything as they looked at me sitting in my wheelchair. They didn't need to. I know I'm considered one of the lowest functioning subjects in a place where the only entry requirement is an IQ of 30 or less.

Despite all these doubts, Virna wouldn't be swayed. A fire of conviction had been lit within her. After telling people again and again that she thought I could understand what was being said to me, she'd spoken to my parents, who had agreed to have me tested. Tomorrow they're taking me to the place where I might finally be offered a key to my prison door.

'You're going to do your best, aren't you?' Virna says now as she looks at me.

I can see she's worried. Doubt flickers across her face like cloud shadows racing across the horizon on a sunny day. I stare back, wishing I could tell her that I'll use every fibre of my being to make the most of an opportunity I never thought would come. This is the first time I've ever been assessed like this and I'll do all I can to give some small sign that I'm worthy of the attention.

'Please do as much as you can, Martin,' Virna says. 'It's so important that you show them what you can do because I know you can.'

I look at her. Tears glimmer silver in the corners of her eyes. Her faith in me is so strong I must repay it.

6

Awakening

Two glass doors slide open in front of me with a hiss. I've never seen doors like this before. The world has surprised me again. I sometimes see it as it passes the window of a car I'm sitting in but other than that I remain separate from it. The small glimpses I have of the world always intrigue me. I once spent days thinking about a doctor's mobile phone after seeing it clipped to his belt: it was so much smaller than Dad's that I couldn't stop wondering what kind of battery was powering it. There are so many things I wish I could understand.

My father is pushing my wheelchair as we enter the Centre for Augmentative and Alternative Communication at the University of Pretoria. It is July 2001 — thirteen and a half years since I first fell ill. On the pavement outside I saw students walking along in the sunshine and jacaranda trees arching overhead but everything is quiet inside the building. Sea-green carpet tiles stretch down a corridor; the walls are covered in information posters. We are a small band of explorers entering this unknown world: my parents, my brother David and Virna, plus Marietta and Elize, a carer and physiotherapist who have known me for years.

'Mr and Mrs Pistorius?' a voice asks and I raise my eyes to see a woman. 'My name is Shakila and I'll be assessing Martin today. We're just getting the room ready but it won't be long.'

Fear washes cold over me. I can't look into the faces around me; I don't want to see the doubt or hope in their eyes as we silently wait. Soon we're ushered into a small room where Shakila is waiting with another woman called Yasmin. I hang my head as they start talking to my parents. The inside of my cheek feels sore. I accidentally bit myself as I was fed my lunch earlier today and my mouth still feels tender even though the bleeding has stopped.

As Shakila asks my parents about my medical history, I wonder what they're thinking after all this time. Do they feel as afraid as I do?

'Martin?' I hear a voice say and my wheelchair is pushed across the room.

We come to rest in front of a large sheet of perspex suspended on a metal stand directly in front of me. Red lines criss-cross the screen, dividing it into boxes with small black and white pictures stuck in some of them. These line drawings show simple things – a ball, a running tap, a dog – and Shakila stands on the other side of the screen watching me intently as I stare at them.

'I want you to look at the picture of the ball, Martin,' Shakila says.

I raise my head a little and let my eyes search the screen.

I can't control my head enough to move it properly from side to side so my eyes are the only part of my body that I'm totally the master of. They slide back and forth across the pictures until I find the ball. I fix my eyes on it and stare.

'Good, Martin, that's very good,' Shakila says softly as she looks at me.

I feel afraid suddenly. Am I looking at the right picture? Are my eyes really fixed on the ball or are they looking at another of the symbols? I can't even be sure of that.

'Now I want you to look at the dog,' Shakila says and I start to search again.

My eyes move slowly over the pictures not wanting to make a mistake or miss a thing. I search slowly until I find the cartoon dog to the left of the board and look at it.

'And now the television,' she says.

I soon find the picture of the television. But although I want to keep staring at it to show Shakila that I've found what she'd asked me to, my chin drops towards my chest. I try not to panic as I wonder if I'm failing the test.

'Shall we try something different?' Shakila asks and my wheelchair is pushed towards a table covered in cards.

Each one has a word and a picture drawn on it. Panic. I can't read the words. I don't know what they say. If I can't read them, will I fail the test? And if I fail the test, will I go back to the care home and sit there forever? My heart starts to thump painfully inside my chest.

'Can you point to the word "Mum" please, Martin?' Yasmin, the other speech therapist, asks me.

I don't know what the word 'Mum' looks like but even so I stare at my right hand, willing it to move, wanting it to make some small sign that I understand what I'm being asked. My hand trembles furiously as I try to lift it from my lap. The room is deathly silent as my arm slowly lifts into the air before jerking wildly from side to side. I hate my arm.

'Let's try again, shall we?' Shakila says.

My progress is painfully slow as I'm asked to identify symbols by pointing at them. I feel ashamed of my useless body and angry that it can't do better the first time anyone asks anything of it.

Soon Shakila goes to a large cupboard and pulls out a small rectangular dial. It has more symbols on it and a large red pointer in the middle. Shakila sets it on the table in front of me before plugging in some wires that run from a yellow plate fixed to the end of a flexible stand.

'This is a dial scan and a head switch,' Yasmin explains. 'You can use the yellow switch to control the pointer on the scan as it goes around and stop it to identify the symbol you want. Do you understand, Martin? Can you see the symbols on the scan?

'When we ask you to identify one, we want you to push your head against the switch when the pointer reaches the symbol. Do you think you can do that?'

I look at the symbols: one shows water running from a tap, another a plate of biscuits, a third a cup of tea. There are eight symbols in total.

'I want you to stop the pointer when it reaches the tap, please,' Yasmin says.

The red pointer starts to inch around the dial. It goes so slowly that I wonder if it'll ever reach the picture of the tap. Slowly it drags its way around the dial and I watch until it nears the tap. I jerk my head against the switch. The pointer stops at the right place on the dial.

'Good, Martin,' a voice tells me.

Amazement fills me. I've never controlled anything before. I've never made another object do what I wanted it to. I've fantasised about it again and again but I've never raised a fork to my mouth, drunk from a cup or changed TV channels. I can't do up my shoes, kick a ball or ride a bike. Stopping the pointer on the dial makes me feel triumphant.

For the next hour, Yasmin and Shakila give me different switches to use as they try to find out if there is any part of my body that I can control enough to use switches properly. My head, knee and rebellious limbs are all put close enough to switches for me to try to make contact with them. First there's a black rectangular box with a long white switch that sits on the side of the table in front of me. It's called a wobble switch. I pull my right arm up before jerking it down, hoping to make contact with the switch and knowing it'll be by luck rather than judgement if I do. Then there is a huge yellow switch, as big and round as a saucer, that I flail my unruly right hand near because my left is almost completely useless. Again and again Yasmin and Shakila ask me to use the switches to iden-tify simple symbols: a knife, a bath, a sandwich – the easiest kind of pictures, which even those with the lowest intelligence can identify. Sometimes I try to use my right hand but more often I stare at the symbol I'm being asked to pick out.

After what feels like forever, Shakila finally turns to me. I'm looking intently at a symbol that shows a big yellow swirl.

'Do you like McDonald's?' she asks.

I don't know what she's talking about. I can't turn my

head or smile to answer yes or no because I don't understand the question.

'Do you like hamburgers?'

I smile at Shakila to let her know that I do and she gets up. Going back to the large cupboard, she pulls out a black box. The top is divided into small squares by an overlying plastic frame and inside each one I can see a symbol.

'This is a communication device called a Macaw,' Shakila tells me softly. 'And if you can learn to use switches, then you might be able to use one of these some day.'

I stare at the box as Shakila turns it on and a tiny red light flashes slowly in the corner of each square in turn. The symbols in the squares aren't black and white like those on the cards. These are brightly coloured and there are words written next to them. I can see a picture of a cup of tea and a drawing of a sun. I watch Shakila to see what will happen next as she hits a switch to select a symbol.

'I am tired,' a recorded voice says suddenly.

It comes from the box. It's a woman's voice. I stare at the Macaw. Could this small black box give me a voice? I can hardly believe that anyone would think me capable of using it. Do they realise I can do more than point at a child's ball drawn in thick black lines on a card?

'I'm sure that you understand us,' Shakila says as she sits in front of me. 'I can see from the way your eyes travel that you can identify the symbols we ask you to and you are trying to use your hand to do the same. I feel sure we'll be able to find a way to help you communicate, Martin.'

I stare at the floor, unable to move any more today.

'Wouldn't you like to be able to tell someone that you are

tired or thirsty?' Shakila says softly. 'That you would like to wear a blue jumper instead of a red one or that you want to go to sleep?'

I'm not sure. I've never told anyone what I want before. Would I be able to make choices if I was given them? Would I be able to tell someone that I want to leave my tea to cool instead of drinking it in hurried gulps when they lift a straw to my mouth because I know it'll be the only opportunity I'll have to drink for several hours? I know most people make thousands of decisions every day about what to eat and wear, where to go and who to see but I'm not sure I'll be able to make even one. It's like asking a child who has grown up in the desert to throw themselves into the sea.

7

My Parents

While my father's faith in me has been stretched almost to breaking point, I don't think it's ever disappeared completely. Its roots were planted deeply many years ago when Dad met a man who'd recovered from polio. It had taken him a decade to get well again but his experience convinced my father that anything was possible. Each day Dad has proved his faith in me in a string of tiny acts: washing and feeding me, dressing and lifting me, getting up every two hours throughout the night to turn my still body. A bear of a man with a huge grey beard like Father Christmas, his hands are always gentle.

It took time for me to realise that while my father looked after nearly all of my physical needs, my mother hardly came near me. Anger and resentment at what had happened poured out of her whenever she did. As time passed I saw that my family had been divided into two — my father and me on one side; my mother, David and Kim on the other — and I realised that my illness had driven a deep wedge into the heart of a family I somehow instinctively knew had once been so happy.

Guilt filled me when I heard my parents arguing. Everyone was suffering because of me. I was the cause of all the bad feeling as my parents returned to the same battleground again and again: my mother wanted to put me into full-time residential care just as the doctors had advised; my father did not. She believed my condition was permanent and I needed so much special care that having me at home would harm David and Kim. My father, on the other hand, still hoped I might get better and believed it would never happen if I was sent away to an institution. This was the fundamental disagreement that reverberated through the years, sometimes as shouts and screams, sometimes as loaded silences.

For a long time I didn't understand why my mother felt so differently to my father but eventually I pieced together enough of the facts to realise that she had almost been destroyed by my illness and she wanted to protect David and Kim from a similar fate. She had lost one child and she didn't want her healthy surviving son and daughter to be hurt in any way.

It hadn't always been this way. For the first two years of my illness, my mother searched as tirelessly as my father for a cure to save the son she thought was dying as he slipped a little more out of their reach every day. I can't imagine how my parents suffered as they watched their healthy child disappear and pleaded with doctors, watched me being given medications and agreed to have me tested for everything from tuberculosis of the brain to a host of genetic disorders only to be told that nothing could help me.

Even when traditional medicine ran out of answers, my mother wasn't prepared to give up. For a year after the doctors told my parents they didn't know how to treat me she cared for me at home and tried everything from having me prayed over by faith healers to intensive vitamin regimes in the hope of helping me. Nothing worked.

My mother was tortured by her growing guilt that she hadn't been able to save me. She was sure she had failed her child and felt increasingly desperate as her friends and family stayed away – some because they found my undiagnosed illness frightening, others because they were unsure how to comfort people who were facing any parents' worst nightmare. Whatever their reason, people kept their distance as they hugged their healthy children close to them in silent gratitude and my family became more and more isolated.

My mother's unhappiness soon spiralled so badly out of control that she tried to commit suicide one night about two years after I first fell ill. After taking handfuls of pills, she lay down to die. But as she did so, Mum remembered what her mother had once told her about her father's sudden death of a heart attack: he'd never said goodbye. Even in her fog of despair, my mother wanted to tell my father one last time how much she loved us all and this saved her. When Dad realised what she'd done, he put her into the car with David, Kim and me, and one of David's friends who was staying the night, and drove us all to the hospital.

The doctors pumped Mum's stomach but after that night my brother's friend was never allowed to stay again and the isolation that my parents felt started to infect my younger brother and sister. They, too, suffered while my mother was treated on a psychiatric ward. By the time she came home, her doctors had decided that she could no longer help care for me. According to them, she was mourning the loss of her child and should have as little as possible to do with me to avoid further upset. She – ill, grief-stricken and desperate – took the doctors at their word and concentrated on caring for her two healthy children and returning to work full-time once she was well enough. Meanwhile, my father held down a demanding job and looked after me, for the most part, single-handedly.

It was like this for many years but gradually the situation has changed as my mother has softened and become more involved in my care. Now she looks after me almost as much as my father does, makes me the spaghetti and mince with peach chutney that she knows I like and sometimes even lays my head on her lap if I'm lying on the sofa. It makes me happy to know that she can touch me now after shying away for so long, just as it makes me sad when I hear her playing music late at night because I know that sorrow is filling her as she listens to lyrics and remembers the past.

Sadness fills me too when I think of my father, who buried his ambitions, lost out on promotions and took demotions to care for me. Each person in my family – my parents, brother and sister – has paid a high price for my illness. While I can't be sure, I sometimes wonder if all these lost hopes and dreams are the reason why a man as intelligent as my father has learned to hide his emotions so deeply that I sometimes wonder if he knows where they are any more.

8

Changes

They call it the butterfly effect: the huge changes that a pair of silken wings can create with an almost imperceptible flutter. I think a butterfly is beating its wings somewhere in my life. To the outward eye, things have hardly changed since I was assessed: I still go to my care centre each morning and sigh gratefully when the afternoon comes to an end and I can go home to be fed, washed and prepared for bed. But monotony is a familiar foe and even the subtlest changes in it are noticeable.

The various care staff I see at my day centre, during appointments for physio or with doctors at the hospital, don't seem overly worried that an expert has said I might soon be able to communicate. Considering some of the things I've seen, I'm surprised some of them aren't a little more concerned. But I can certainly feel a change in the way my parents are speaking to me since I was assessed by the speech therapists. When Mum asks if I've had enough food, she waits just a little longer for my head to jerk its way down or my mouth to smile. My father talks to me more and more now as he brushes my teeth at night. The changes are so small that my parents might not even be aware of them but I can sense hope in the air for the first time in years.

I've heard enough of what they've said to know that if I'm to start communicating properly it will be at the most basic level. This will not be a Hollywood movie with a neat happy ending or a trip to Lourdes where the mute are miraculously given a voice. The speech therapists' report has recommended that my mother and father start trying to communicate with me in the tiniest of ways. Apparently my head-jerk and smile are not as reliable as I thought they were and I must learn a more consistent way to signal yes and no. Because my hands are too unruly to point properly, the best way for me to start 'speaking' is by staring at symbols.

I'll use symbols because I can't read or write. Letters hold no meaning for me now, and so pictures will rule my life from now on: I'm going to live and breathe them as I learn their language. My parents have been told to make me a folder of words and their corresponding symbols. 'Hello' is a picture of a stick man waving his hand, 'like' is his face up close with a huge grin and 'thank you' is a drawing of an egg-shaped face with two hands held flat just below the mouth.

Once Mum and Dad have made up all the pages telling people my name and where I live, that I would like my jumper put on or to be moved out of the way of the sun, they can put them in my folder. Then the person I'm speaking to can slowly turn the pages and I'll stare extra hard at the symbol I want to choose. If I need to let my parents know at mealtimes that my food is too hot, cold or bland, I can stare at one of the laminated pieces of A4 paper they've been advised to stick onto my place mat.

Of course no one has any idea how much of this I can understand because they've never tried to do anything like it with me before. During my assessment, I showed that I can obey simple commands – but so can a toddler. That's why I must start with small steps and hope the people teaching me will soon realise I'm capable of more.

It'll take time but at least there is one way I'll be able to show people I understand things they haven't considered before. Babies might eat puréed food day after day without complaint but I'll soon be able to ask someone to pass me the salt. For the first time in my life, I'll be able to season my food.

9

The Beginning and the End

The care home I've attended since I fell ill is called Alpha and Omega, the beginning and the end. But there isn't too much of either to be found here for me because I'm trapped in a purgatory of bland days, which ebb one into the other.

The centre is housed in a single-storey building with two bright and airy classrooms, a small physiotherapy room and a garden. Sometimes I'm wheeled out into the sunshine but usually I stay inside, where I'm moved from a sitting position in my chair to lying on a mat on the floor. Mostly I'm rested on my side or back but occasionally I'm put face down on a large cushioned wedge so that a care worker can encourage me to try lifting my head by tapping it with the palm of their hand. Otherwise I lie inert, looking at mint-green walls and listening to the tinny chirpiness of the television or radio that provides a constant backdrop to my days. I prefer it when the radio is on because trying to watch the television requires effort that I often can't muster. Instead I stare at the brown carpet tiles and listen to footsteps clicking on the lino floor in the corridor outside.

Classroom language is used here but I'm not sure why because none of the children are thought to be educable. Whatever the reason, my fellow inmates and I have 'teachers' and are divided into two 'classes', which are randomly changed every so often. Sometimes we are split into children-who-can-walk and children-who-can't; at other times it's a question of dividing up those who don't get on. Once we were even separated according to IQ, although when everyone's is considered to be 30 or under it seemed a bit like splitting hairs to me.

Usually about half a dozen staff, who look after us each day, do activities such as stretching our legs or covering our hands in paint before pressing them onto pieces of paper. A couple of the children can join in a little but most are like me and can't control their movements enough to do anything. I've often wondered who these activities are supposed to benefit as I've sat having my hand smeared with cold red paint before it is dragged across a sheet of paper: us or our parents? Are we being forced to collude in a necessary lie when a member of staff draws a picture using our hand? I've seen so many parents being given a drawing they must know their child couldn't have done but none of them says a word as they stare at it.

I've only ever heard one mother question whether her son actually produced the painting and the carer gave her a silent smile when she did, as if pleading with her not to crack the façade of false optimism that has been built around us. I understand why parents want a strand of hope to cling on to, however fragile, just as I understand why such activities might be enjoyable for those children who find being touched and spoken to a relief from a monotonous day, but mostly I wish I could be left alone.

I'm usually trying to listen to the radio when someone comes to disturb me with a smile. I know they mean well, of course, but I'm the oldest here and the activities are aimed at much younger children. No one seems to consider that even people who are thought to be intellectually impaired can change as they grow older.

Despite all this, I know from experience that Alpha and Omega is a far better care centre than many. Over the years I've often heard people talking in shocked whispers about what they've seen at other places. They're right to be shocked. I've seen things for myself: I was sent to other homes when my father went away on business because my mother wasn't confident about looking after me alone, and when my family had a holiday because they needed a break from caring for me.

Each time I was left, I felt terrified I would never be taken home again and my anxiety would build day by day as fear took control of me. On the day I was due to be picked up, each minute felt like a year as I waited to hear the familiar voices of my mother and father. My greatest fear is that I will be left in one of those places where children like me sit all day with no interaction or stimulation. That would be the worst kind of living death.

So I'm grateful to the staff here, who at least try to give our lives a little more texture, because working in a place like this is not everyone's cup of tea. I've lost count of the carers I've seen come and go over the years. Many disappear almost as soon as they arrive and I've learned how to recognise the look of almost revolted confusion they get before even they realise they feel that way. I understand. Some people are scared by what they can't comprehend. It makes them uncomfortable to see the elfin features of a child with Down's syndrome, the twisted limbs of one with cerebral palsy or the unseeing stare of an infant with brain damage.

But for all the people who can't bear to look after the children here, there are some for whom this work is a calling. First among them is Rina, the principal of the home, who has a round, smiling face and taught me one of my earliest lessons about the people who care for me.

Years ago, when Rina was a teacher instead of being in charge, she became very attached to a little girl called Sally who had been born with severe cerebral palsy. Rina adored Sally: she fed her the gem squash she loved, cradled her tightly in her arms and played the music that always made her smile. Rina was so close to the little girl, in fact, that she was at the hospital on the night Sally died of pneumonia, aged six.

After that, some of the light went out of Rina's eyes and seeing how bitterly she missed Sally taught me that children like myself could be so much more than just a job. It has been a comforting thought to carry with me throughout the years and all the meetings with people who have treated me like little more than a carcass to be handled as a chicken is manoeuvred into the pot. Not a shred of human warmth melts their chilly professionalism. Humping you like a sack of potatoes, they wash you briskly with freezing water and always get soap in your eyes, however hard you squeeze them shut, before thoughtlessly feeding you food that is either too cold or too hot. All the while they don't speak a word or smile for fear of seeing a person staring back.

Worse though are the so-called carers whose callousness becomes far more personal. I've been called 'the obstacle', 'donkey' and 'rubbish' by people who assume they're superior but in so doing show just how stupid they really are. Do they think that a limited intellect means a child can't feel viciousness in a person's touch or hear anger in the tone of their voice? I remember, in particular, the rush of cold air that always used to wake me when one woman impatiently ripped off my blanket as I slept each afternoon and the temporary worker who threw me into a chair so roughly that I fell out of it as it tipped forwards and dived head first onto the floor.

Such experiences aside, I've come to the conclusion that there are more good people than bad looking after children like me because when I look back over the years I see a stream of smiling faces. There was Unna, who always seemed to be sweating because her nose was permanently shiny, and Heila, who pulsed with such anxious energy that even her tongue couldn't stop moving as she nervously licked her lips. Today there's Marietta, who loves *Days of Our Lives* and has a fiery temper under her calm exterior; Helen, who giggles as she tickles me and has fingernails with a dark-brown stripe down the middle that I can never stop staring at; and my own personal favourite, Dora – middle-aged, plump and smiling, her calmness reassures me and kindness makes her eyes a soft, liquid brown.

However different they are, the one thing all these women have in common is a love of chatting and gossiping, exchanging news and sympathising with each other's troubles. I've heard stories of snakes that have slithered into houses at night and been beaten to death by a brave husband, tales of water leaks that made it rain inside and threatened to bring down ceilings and descriptions of grandchildren bouncing furiously up and down on beds whenever a certain song is played. I also know about the trials of coping with a parent who has Alzheimer's, the problems of caring for sick relatives and the difficulties of getting maintenance from an unwilling ex-husband.

Whatever else they talk about, though, I've come to know that there are three topics women will return to again and again in conversation: their husbands, who are often a disappointment; their children, who are usually wonderful; and their weight, which is always too high. Again and again, I hear them commiserate with each other about how difficult it is to make men more responsible and diets more effective. While I don't understand their problems with their husbands, my heart always sinks whenever I hear them talk about calorie counting. Women seem to think they go on diets in order to feel happier, but I know from experience that this isn't true. In fact, I can safely say that the less women eat, the grumpier they get.

10

Day by Day

Life is finally starting to happen to me as my parents discuss how best to help me. Their ambitions for me now extend far beyond paper symbols and they have decided to buy me an electronic communication device like the black box we saw at my assessment. It is a leap of faith that I wish I could thank them for. They still have no idea if I'll be able to use such a device but they are willing to try because the small spark of hope ignited by my assessment has lit a fire within them.

Together we are discovering a new world called Augmentative and Alternative Communication, or AAC. It's the place where the mute can find a voice through everything from the most basic forms of communication, such as pointing, blinking or staring at symbols held up by another person, to high-tech speech-generating devices and computer programmes that one person uses alone.

To operate a device independently, I must be able to use

switches, so my mother takes me back to see Shakila and a physiotherapist called Jill. After testing me again, they identify the two switches I might best be able to use: one, called a lolly switch, is a small rectangular box that sits in my palm and is operated by curling my fingers to press the button; the other is a wobble switch, which is long enough for my inaccurate right hand to connect with sometimes if I flail it in the right direction.

At first I was overwhelmed with excitement when my parents decided to buy me a device. But then frustration filled me as I realised the black box could only store about 250 words and phrases. It does not seem like much to say when the words inside me feel so limitless.

But then South African currency suddenly devalues and my parents have to cancel the order for the device after it almost doubles in price. Instead they decide to buy me a computer that can be loaded with communication software. It's a brave decision because no one else in South Africa uses one. Speech therapists won't be able to help us – no one will. If I'm to learn anything it will be entirely down to me and my parents, and they don't even know if I'm capable of using a computer.

For now, they must decide what software to buy me and whatever they choose could change things for me completely. It is nerve-racking but exhilarating. My emotions jostle for space like baby birds in a nest: excitement at the thought of learning to communicate, guilt that I'm happy I won't be getting the black box and remorse I feel this way when my parents showed such faith in me by ordering the device. Each feeling is different: excitement makes my stomach shiver, guilt brings a soft swell of nausea deep inside and remorse makes my heart feel heavy. These emotions are so different to what I've known for so long – feelings that I muted to grey to save myself from being driven mad by my powerlessness over every identical day.

'Hello, boy,' my father says when he walks into my room at 6 a.m. each morning.

Dad is always dressed by the time he gets me up. Then he washes me and puts on my clothes before wheeling me into the kitchen, where I'm fed a bowl of cereal. I'm also given a cup of coffee, which I drink through a straw. By the time it's finished I know we'll soon be leaving for the care centre. Dad drops me off on his way to work each morning and the final thing he does before leaving the house is to put a bag onto my lap containing the clean clothes, incontinence pads and bibs I'll need for the day, plus a cooler bag with all my food and drinks.

The moment the front door opens is always a tiny thrill for me. Wondering what the weather will be like is one of the few unpredictable elements of my day, after all. Will there be a snap in the air or a cloudy sky? Given that the sun shines a lot here, it isn't usually much of a surprise but I revel in those few short moments of suspense as my father opens the door.

After Dad puts me into the car and folds my wheelchair into the boot, he gets in beside me, switches on the radio and we drive without speaking. Half an hour later, we reach the care home, where he gets me out of the car again and puts me back into my wheelchair. Then Dad lays my bag on my lap and wheels me to the brown gate that secures the entrance to

Alpha and Omega. As he pushes me down the corridor to my classroom and my wheelchair comes to a halt, I know that I'm going to be left for another day. It's usually between 7.15 and 8.10 a.m. by the time Dad leaves, which means I'll have to wait for anything up to eleven hours until I see him again.

'Bye, boy,' he says as he bends down to kiss me and I hear his footsteps disappearing as he walks back up the corridor.

The days at the care home don't really start properly until about 9.30 a.m., so I sit in my chair until then or sometimes I'm put onto a bean-bag, which I prefer because it supports my body so well. Then I lie or sit for the rest of the morning and sometimes I'm lifted up to do stretching exercises or an activity. After a mid-morning cup of tea, I'm sometimes taken outside for fresh air, and ninety minutes later it's time for lunch, which is the same every day – stewed fruit and yoghurt followed by orange or guava squash. Then at midday someone lies me down to sleep with the other children and three precious hours are lost until I'm woken up for my afternoon drink and put into my wheelchair again to wait for Dad.

I often find this part of the day hard because, although the centre officially closes at 5.15 p.m., Dad doesn't usually arrive until sometime between 5.20 and 6.30 p.m. because he can't leave work early and often gets held up in rush-hour traffic. Some of the staff don't like it and I often overhear conversations criticising him. It upsets me each time because I know my father is doing the best he can.

'Hello, boy,' he says with a smile when he finally walks into my classroom and I breathe a sigh of relief because I've finally reached the end of another day.

Then my bag is put back onto my lap, I'm wheeled to the

car, my chair is stowed in the boot once more and we drive home listening to the radio. After pulling into the driveway and going inside, we usually find Mum cooking, then we sit around the dining-room table to eat before I'm given a cup of milky coffee and laid on the sofa in the lounge in front of the TV. Most nights my father falls asleep in his armchair while he watches a programme, then he wakes up, puts me back into my chair, wheels me to the bathroom to brush my teeth and puts me into bed after undressing me.

The only change to the routine comes at weekends, when I get to stay at home and am given a lie-in until I'm lifted out of bed and taken to the lounge, where I spend the day lying or sitting. But at least my family are around me and I get to hear everyone talking. These are the days that always give me strength for another week because I love being with my parents and David – Kim too before she moved to the UK. That is why sadness always fills me when my father washes my hair as he bathes me on Sunday nights and prepares me to start another week at the care centre. Every second or third week, he cuts my nails and I hate having that done.

This is the routine of my life and has been for as long as I can remember. So is it any wonder that I hang on to every word my parents say as they discuss what to do and I begin to dream of a future I never thought I would have?

II

The Wretch

It was Virna alone who offered me safe passage from my silent self after we first met three years ago. Unlike the people who are now trying to reach me with symbols and dials, switches and screens, Virna only ever used intuition. Like a master detective following the clues I sometimes inadvertently left, she never looked for one conclusive piece of evidence. Instead she was content to piece together a string of tiny fragments to make a whole.

It took time. I wasn't willing at first to see that someone wanted to communicate with me. I was scared to believe someone might. But when I realised that Virna wasn't going to give up, I gradually opened up and over the months and years that followed we became friends.

'How are you today, Martin?' she'd ask as she walked into the tiny room at Alpha and Omega where she massaged me once a week.

Lying on my back, I'd watch as she unzipped the small bag

filled with oils that she always carried with her. As I heard the sound of a bottle being opened, I'd wait to see what smell would fill the air. Sometimes it was citrus, sometimes mint or eucalyptus, but each time the fragrance hit my nostrils I was taken from Kansas to Oz.

'I'm going to do your legs first today and then I'll do your back,' Virna tells me. 'We haven't done it for a couple of weeks and I'm sure it must be sore.'

She looks at me with her enquiring eyes. Virna is small and slight with a voice to match and I've always known she is a kind person. I could hear it the first time she spoke to me and feel it in the healing fingertips that worked muscles long knotted by disuse.

My heart swells as I look at Virna. We have forty-five minutes together now and, just as a child counts out shells collected on a day at the beach, I will go through each one again. I must take care not to rush through these moments. Instead I will slow each one down so that I can replay them because they are what sustain me now. Virna is the only one who sees me. More importantly, she believes in me. She understands my language – the smiles, gazes and nods that are all I have at my disposal.

'Is your family well?' Virna asks as she massages me.

My eyes follow her as I lie on my back. I keep my face still to let her know that someone is sick.

'Is your father ill?'

I don't respond.

'Your mother?'

Again nothing.

'Is it David?'

I give Virna a half smile to show that she is right.

'David is poorly then,' she says. 'What is it? Does he have a cold?'

I jerk my head down.

'Tonsilitis?'

I give another twitch of my feeble neck but it is enough for Virna to understand. Moving down through ear, nose and throat, she finally reaches the chest and I give her another half smile.

'He's got a chest infection?'

I knit my eyebrows to let her know that she is almost right.

'Not pneumonia?' she asks.

I push air sharply through my nose.

'What else is there?'

We stare at each other.

'Bronchitis?' Virna says at last.

Happiness surges through me as I smile. I am Muhammad Ali, John McEnroe, Fred Trueman. Crowds are roaring their approval as I take a lap of honour in the stadium. Virna smiles back at me. She understands. I will replay this moment again and again until we next meet because this one – and the others like it – puncture the shroud of invisibility that has been wrapped around me.

Virna even inspired others to talk to me more – in particular, my sister Kim. I always knew that she looked after me: feeding me gravy she'd saved from her plate because she knew I liked it, bringing Pookie to sit on my lap or pushing my wheelchair close to her while she watched TV. But after Kim realised that I was responding to Virna, she started to talk to me more – telling me about her life the way any sister might tell her older brother. She spoke to me about what was happening at university and the coursework she was worried about as she trained to become a social worker, or the friends who had made her happy and the ones who hadn't. Kim didn't know it, of course, but I understood every word and thought my heart might burst with happiness as I watched her walk up to accept her degree. Other than Virna, she was the one person who could interpret what I was trying to communicate at times, guessing what I liked and didn't like better than most.

That's why I've missed Kim so much since she moved to England a year ago but at least I still have Virna. In a life where people talk relentlessly about my physical needs – am I hot or cold, tired or hungry? – she sees me as more than an empty vessel. And now Kim is no longer here to hug me, Virna is the only person who touches me in anything but a perfunctory way. Others wash and wipe, dress and dust me down but it's always as a means to an end. Only Virna touches me for no other reason than to soothe my aching body – she comforts and heals, making me feel like something other than the repulsive creature I know I am.

I understand that people don't touch me affectionately because they are scared to. I'm a little scared of myself if truth be told. When I catch sight of my reflection in the mirror, I quickly look away because staring back at me is a man with glazed eyes, a bib to catch his drool and arms that are drawn up to his chest like a dog begging for bones. I hardly recognise this stranger so I understand if other people find him hard to stomach. Years ago I went to a family party where I heard one of my relatives talk about me as I sat in the corner.

'Look at him,' she said sadly. 'Poor thing. What kind of life is that?'

Embarrassment flooded through me as the woman looked away. She couldn't bear to look at me and I knew I was ruining whatever pleasure she might have taken from the party. It wasn't surprising. How could anyone enjoy themselves when confronted with such a wretched sight?

12

Life and Death

I'm poised to bury the first crampons in the rockface of communication. The switches I'll use to operate the computer which will speak for me have arrived and I've started practising with them, knowing they are so much more than nuts and bolts, discs of plastic or networks of electric wires. Talking, chatting, arguing, joking, gossiping, conversing, negotiating, chitchatting: these are all within my reach now thanks to the switches. Praising, questioning, thanking, requesting, complimenting, asking, complaining and discussing: they are almost at my disposal too.

First we must decide which software programme to buy so my parents order various demonstation CDs from Europe and America to test out. Weeks turn into months as my mother spends hours looking at website pages loading slowly on the Internet while my father devotes his evenings to reading information he has printed during his day at work.

As I watch and listen, I begin to understand what will help

me best express myself. Like an artist mixing paint to just the right consistency for his canvas, I must choose the right software. Now, nearly six months after I was first assessed, my parents urge me to tell them what I want. They're asking me because they've seen that I don't hang my head like a beaten dog any more now there's something interesting to look at. Hope rises off my mother and father like steam from a scalding bath as they begin to see tiny signs of what I might be capable of.

I can't stop thinking about how my life will change once we finally decide which software to buy. The thought that I might soon hear my 'voice' say 'I'm hungry' as many times as I want it to astounds me. Realising that I might be able to ask 'What's on the TV?' amazes me. These simple words are my own personal Mount Everests and to think I might soon conquer them is almost unimaginable.

I find myself drawn back to certain symbols that I look at in wonder. 'Who' is represented by a blank face with a question mark on it and 'what' is a square with a question mark inside. These are the building blocks of questions I haven't been able to ask. 'I want' is represented by a pair of hands reaching towards a red block, while two parallel thick black lines mean 'I am'. This is the symbol I return to perhaps more than any other because I am so unsure of what to say after those two small words. I am ... What? Who? I don't know. I've never been given a chance to find out.

Before I begin to answer those questions, I must master the basics of any sentence – single words and their symbols. Juice, tea, sugar, milk, hello, goodbye, I, you, we, they, no, yes, chicken, chips, meat, and, hair, mouth, bread, goodbye: only once I've learned these can I start to put them together to make sentences.

'I would like orange juice.'

'No, thank you.'

'I'm hungry.'

'I would like to go to bed.'

'I am cold.'

'I would like radishes and toast with jam.'

First, though, I must show my parents which software programme I want by nodding my head when they read out the names, but it feels impossible to decide. Again and again they've asked me but I can't bring myself to choose and we've been stuck in the doldrums of indecision for weeks now.

'Sometimes in life you just have to move forward,' my father told me a few days ago. 'You have to make a decision and stick with it. We just want you to show us which software you'd like us to buy. We're pretty sure you know which one you want, Martin.'

He looks at me as I stare mutely back at him.

'This is just the start,' Dad says softly. 'It isn't life and death.'

But it feels like it to me.

I've never made decisions before and now I must make the hardest one of all. How do you pick the bridge you will use to travel from one world into another? This software isn't just a piece of equipment: it will be my voice. What if I make the wrong choice? What if I pick something that limits me too much or is too complex for me to use? If I make a mistake, I might never get this chance again.

'We can buy something else if we don't get it right at first,' my mother tells me.

But her reassurances don't soothe away my terrors. Even as one part of me wonders how far my parents' faith will stretch – if I can't use the software, will they give up the wild dream the sceptics around us think will never come true – I find myself questioning what it will mean if all goes well and my world starts to open up. My parents might now believe I'm capable of more than anyone thought possible, as they've watched my right hand get a little steadier with the switches and seen me speed up as I practise selecting symbols, but they still don't completely understand. What will happen to us if the world we've known for so long changes to the extent that it tips off its axis? I'm so used to a cage that I don't know if I'll be able to see the open horizon even when I'm staring at it.

As doubts and anxiety fill me, I force myself to think of a telephone call my parents and David made to Kim a few weeks ago at Christmas. As they chatted, I sat nervously in front of my parents' computer and my hands shook even more than usual as I slowly clicked on symbols. Then my father held the phone close to the computer speakers and I pressed the switch for a final time.

'Hello, Kim,' my disembodied computer voice said. 'Happy Christmas.'

There was silence for a moment before my sister spoke but then I heard the joy in her voice from almost six thousand miles away. And in that moment I knew the ghost boy was finally coming back to life.

13

My Mother

Frustration flickers across my mother's face as she stares at me. I know this look well. Sometimes her features become so still that her face almost freezes. We're working at the computer together as we try to add words to my growing vocabulary. It's August 2002, a year since I was first assessed, and we've been learning to use my communication system for about six months. Kim brought the software with her on a visit from the UK after I finally decided what I wanted and I even have my own laptop now after Mum took me to buy one.

'These are all too old,' she said purposefully as she looked at the laptops lined up like gravestones in a computer shop. 'I want the newest one you have – top of the range, please. It must be quick and powerful. My son mustn't have any problems with it.'

Once again I watched her negotiate for me just as I'd seen her do so many times over the years. In her firm but polite manner, I've seen Mum insist to doctors who've said I was well that they must examine me again and argue with other medics who've wanted to put me at the back of the queue. Now she was going to make sure I got the best laptop the shop had to offer.

I hardly dared touch the laptop at first and simply stared at it whenever Dad, Mum or David switched it on. Listening in awe to the music that played like magic when the black screen burst into life, I'd wonder how I was ever going to learn to control this strange machine when I didn't even understand the keyboard. Letters might be just another kind of symbol but, unlike the pictures I'd spent so much time getting to know over the past few months, I don't know how to read them.

Just as you choose the words you speak naturally, I must pick what I want my new computer 'voice' to say by selecting words from grids – or pages – of vocabulary. My software came with very little pre-programmed so now my mother and I must input every word I want in my vocabulary and its corresponding symbol. Then I will be able to use my switches to move the words around and select what I want to say on-screen before the computer voices it.

Today my mother and I are working on words about colour because, just as she did when I was a child, she is helping me learn a new language. Mum has even given up her job as a radiographer to teach me intensively and we work together for several hours every day now when she comes to pick me up from the care centre at about 2 p.m. After going home, we work on building grids for about four hours before she leaves me to practise using them alone.

I know the speed with which I'm learning has surprised

her. At first, she had to teach herself how to use the software before showing me. But as time has gone on, she's seen that I can complete every task she gives me and trusts me to do more. So instead of sitting and reading the computer manuals alone, Mum now reads them to me and I commit everything she says to memory as we learn together. More and more, I seem to understand the instructions better than she does and there are times when I have to wait until she realises what she's doing wrong. But there is nothing I can do to tell her because, despite all my progress, I'm still communicating using only the most basic words and phrases.

Now I look at Mum as she stares at me before turning to the screen. So far today we've added the colours of the rainbow to my new grid – red, yellow, pink, green, purple and orange – as well as the other most obvious choices like blue, black and brown. But it's getting harder now that we're moving into the further reaches of the colour spectrum.

'Cerise?' Mum asks.

I keep my face still.

'Emerald?'

I know exactly what word I want. We often reach an impasse like this as we build a grid.

'Magenta?'

I don't respond in any way.

'Navy?'

For a moment, frustration builds inside me. It claws at the back of my throat as I wish my mother could guess the word I want because, if she can't, I'll never be able to say it. I'm entirely dependent on her to suggest every word I want added to my new vocabulary.

Sometimes there are ways to show the word I'm thinking of and earlier I used a switch to click on the symbol showing an ear and then the one bearing the picture of a sink.

'Sounds like sink?' Mum asked. 'Do you want pink?'

I smiled and the word was added to my grid. Now there's just one more shade I want – turquoise. As Mum runs through the spectrum, I wonder how I'll describe the colour of a summer sky if she doesn't think of it.

While it's frustrating for me, I sometimes wonder if my mother's desire to find the words I want is even more powerful than my own. She is as consumed by this process as I am and never seems to tire of sitting with me at the computer for hour after hour, day after day. When we aren't working together, my mother carries around pieces of paper on which she scribbles word lists as she thinks about the next grid we'll build and the words I might want to add to it. Because the more we work, the more she realises how extensive my vocabulary is, and I can see the shock in her eyes as she realises how much I know.

I think she's beginning to realise how underestimated I've always been but I've no idea how it makes her feel. I suspect it might horrify her to think that I've been fully aware for years but we don't talk about it and I don't think we ever will. Does she see my rehabilitation as a penance for sins of the past? I can't be sure but in her urgency and dedication to me, I wonder if she is fending off memories of those dark years after I first fell ill and the countless arguments when David, Kim and Pookie would disappear and I'd be left sitting in the corner.

'Look at us!' my mother would scream at my father.

'We're a mess. Martin needs special care that we can't give him and I don't understand why you won't let him have it.'

'Because he needs to be here with us,' my father would roar back, 'not with strangers.'

'But think of David and Kim. What about them? David used to be such an outgoing little boy but he's getting more and more withdrawn. And I know Kim seems brave but she needs more of your attention than she gets. She wants to spend time with her father but you're always so busy with Martin. Between him and work you never get a chance to be with the rest of us.'

'Well, that's how it has to be because I'm the only one looking after Martin, aren't I? I'm sorry, Joan, but we're a family and he's part of it. We can't just send him away. We've got to stay together.'

'Why, Rodney? Whose sake are you keeping him here for? Yours, Martin's or ours? Why can't you just accept that we can't look after him?'

'He would be better off somewhere being cared for properly by people who are experts. We could visit him and Kim and David would be so much happier.'

'But I want him here. I can't let him go.'

'And what about me, Kim and David? This isn't doing any of us any good. It's too much.'

On and on the fight would go, spiralling out of control as each battled with the other to win the war and I would listen to it all, knowing I was the cause, wishing I could be in some safe, dark place where I never had to listen to this argument again.

Sometimes, after a particularly bad row, Mum would storm

out of the room but one night Dad put me into the car before driving away. As I wondered if we'd ever go home again, I was filled with guilt about what I'd done to my family. It was my fault this was happening to them. If I'd died, everyone would have been better off. Eventually we went home, of course, and the familiar stony silence that always followed a row calcified around us again.

But there was one fight I'll never forget because after Dad had stormed out, Mum was left crying on the floor. She was wringing her hands, moaning, and I could feel the raw grief flowing out of her: she looked so alone, so confused and desperate. I wished I could reassure her, stand up from my wheelchair and leave behind this shell of a body that had caused so much pain.

Mum looked up at me. Her eyes were filled with tears.

'You must die,' she said slowly as she looked at me. 'You have to die.'

The rest of the world felt so far away when she said those words, and I stared blankly as she got up and left me in the silent room. I wanted to do as she bid me that day. I longed to leave my life because hearing those words was more than I could bear.

As time passed, I gradually learned to understand my mother's desperation, because as I sat in the care home and listened to other parents talk, I discovered many others felt just as tormented as she did. Little by little I learned why it was so hard for my mother to live with such a cruel parody of the once healthy child she had loved so much. Every time she looked at me she could see only the ghost boy he'd left behind.

My mother was far from alone in having these feelings of darkness and desperation. A couple of years after she spoke to me that night, a baby called Mark started coming to the care centre and his learning difficulties were so severe that he had to be tube fed, never made a sound and wasn't expected to survive for long. I never saw him because he lay in a cot all day but I could hear him. I knew what his mother sounded like too because, although I was usually lying on the floor when she came in with Mark, I became familiar with her voice. That's how I heard a conversation she had with Rina one morning.

'There's a moment every morning when I wake up and I don't remember,' Mark's mother said. 'I feel so light inside, so free. Then reality comes crashing back and I think of Mark, another day, another week, as I wonder if he's suffering and how long he might live.

'But I don't get out of bed to go to him straight away. Instead I lie there, looking at the light coming through the window, the curtains blowing in the breeze and each morning I know that I'm building up the courage to go and look in my own son's cot.'

Mark's mother wasn't fighting fate any more. She had accepted the inevitability of her son's death and now waited each morning for it to come, unsure how she'd feel when it did. Neither she nor my mother was a monster – they were just afraid. I long ago learned to forgive Mum for her mistakes. But as I look at her now, her brow knitting in concentration as she tries so hard to think of the colour I want to add to a grid, I wonder if she's forgiven herself. I hope so.

14

Other Worlds

When I needed to forget, I could always be free. However desperate I felt, there was always one place where I knew I could lose myself: my imagination. There I could be anything I wanted to be.

Once I was a pirate boy, stealing onto an enemy ship to take back the gold that had been stolen from my father. I could hear laughter as I climbed up a rope ladder onto the ship and jumped silently onto the wooden deck. A pirate was in the crow's nest far above me, looking out to sea through a telescope – he didn't know an enemy was creeping aboard right under his nose. At the other end of the deck I could see a group of pirates huddled together. They were crouching over a map, passing around a bottle of rum and laughing as they wondered which ship they'd attack next, whose gold they'd steal this time.

I licked my finger and stuck it into the air to find out which way the wind was blowing. I had to make sure the pirates didn't sniff me out because they tied up their prisoners and left them for the birds to pick out their eyes before making them walk the plank. Flinging myself onto the deck, I pulled myself along on my elbows, sliding forward silently, knowing my cutlass was by my side if I needed it. I was ready to slice off the head of any pirate who came too close but they were all too busy staring at their map to notice me. Without a sound, I climbed down the ladder into the ship. I had to find the pirate king's cabin because that was where my father's gold would be.

I came to a door and pushed it open. The pirate king was asleep in a chair but I could tell that he was so tall his head would nearly touch the ceiling if he stood up. He had a big black beard and a patch over one eye, and he was wearing a captain's hat. In front of him was a chest filled with jewels and money, precious stones and cups, and I crept towards it as I scanned the treasure. Then I saw it – the brown leather bag that held my father's gold. It was half hidden underneath a pile of coins and I pulled it carefully, inching it out bit by bit, careful not to make a sound until it was safely in my hand.

I could have left as quietly as I'd arrived, but I didn't.

I walked around the desk to where the pirate king was sitting. His nose was big and red and there was a scar running down his cheek. A parrot, blue and green and yellow, sat on a perch beside him. I fed it some bread from my pocket to keep it quiet before leaning forward and snatching the pirate king's hat as I started to laugh. He opened his good eye and saw me.

'AAAAAAAAAAAAAAARGH!' he roared and I laughed at him even harder.

He leaped up and drew his sword but I was too fast for him. I pushed his hat onto my head, ran for the door and smashed it closed behind me. I could hear the sound of wood splitting as the pirate king kicked his leg through the door and got stuck. Ha! He wouldn't be able to come after me now.

'Thief!' he screamed.

I pulled out my cutlass and pointed it in front of me. It was made of silver so shiny that the sun bounced off it as I ran onto the deck. The pirates were waiting for me but I twisted the cutlass and the light shining off my blade blinded them. They fell to their knees, screaming as they covered their eyes, and I ran to the side of the boat as one of the pirates tried to follow me. I could hear his sword swishing in the air; I could feel him close by. He wanted to catch me for the birds.

I spun around and my cutlass clashed against metal. The pirate's sword flew out of his hand and across the deck as I jumped onto the rigging, still holding my father's gold. I was the pirate boy. I could run and swim, steal and fight, face and outwit my enemies. I smiled as the pirates rushed at me.

'You'll never catch me,' I yelled as I jump off the rigging.

I fell down and down, my body diving like an arrow into the deep blue water, which closed over me. I knew the sea would safely carry me far away. I'd find my father and fight another day. I was the pirate boy and no one's prisoner.

That is where I went to escape the feelings that threatened to overwhelm me when I thought I'd be trapped forever. Now I sometimes wish I could retreat there again as I begin to experience an exquisite torture of hope, frustration, fear and joy as I reconnect with the world. Deep down I know, of course, that I no longer need to lose myself in fantasy because I'm living life at last. But I'll always be thankful for my imagination because I learned long ago that it was my greatest gift: it was the key that unlocked my prison and allowed me to escape, the door through which I entered new worlds and conquered them – the place where I was free.

15

Fried Egg

The band around my head feels tight this morning as I practise on my computer. At its centre is a small black dot, which I'm trying to use to shine an infrared beam on the computer screen with a slight turn of my head. Pressing my feeble hands into one of my switches enables me to choose the word I want to say. This gadget is supposed to help speed up the communicating process but it's taking a long time to learn how to use it.

The desire to master my communication system is all-consuming as I try to control my switches and remember where the symbols we've inputted into my computer are within the word grids. Most days I still go to the care centre for a few hours to give my mother some time to herself, but instead of losing myself in fantasies now, I flick through mental images of the grids to test myself on how to find my way from one to the other, and remember where particular words are stored. When I get home, I work for six, seven, eight hours, sometimes wasting words just to hear myself 'speak'. Like a child in a sweet shop, I gorge myself: verbs are my chocolate bon-bons, nouns are my sticky toffees, adverbs are my jelly sweets and adjectives are my liquorice allsorts. In bed at night, I see symbols running through my head and into my dreams.

Now I watch as each individual word cell on the grid in front of me is highlighted one by one. It contains words about breakfast and the other symbols I've already selected for the sentence are hovering at the top of the screen. 'I would like', 'orange juice', 'and', 'coffee', 'please' stand patiently like a queue of passengers hoping to see a bus they fear might never turn the corner because they've been waiting for so long. Each time I select a symbol, I must wait for the cursor to go back to the beginning of the grid and click slowly through each word cell again. Now I wait because I want to ask my mother for a fried egg for breakfast this morning as well as coffee and juice.

A picture of a steaming cup – 'instant coffee' – is illuminated. Then a picture of a carton – 'milk'.

Honey.

Toast.

Muffin.

Marmite.

Porridge.

Strawberry.

Apricot.

Marmalade.

Jam.

Butter.

Margarine.

Grapefruit.

Orange.

Banana.

Raisin Bread.

There's just one more line of words to go.

I watch as 'omelette', 'tomato' and 'sausage' are highlighted. The cursor moves to the line beginning with 'bacon' and ending with 'fried egg'. That's the symbol I want. I revel in the knowledge that I can now be so specific when I ask for food. Scrambled eggs won't do nor will poached – I want sunny side up, a disc of sunshine yellow to brighten my plate.

I curl my right hand around my lolly switch in readiness. The right one is my most useful hand, the hand I trust. I will ask it now to do as I wish.

The cursor moves on and each cell is highlighted for a few seconds before the next is lit up. 'Egg' and 'scrambled egg' are left behind as the cursor moves forwards. 'Fried egg' is coming up. It nestles between 'poached' and 'boiled'. I wait to pounce on it.

At last. The symbol is illuminated. But as I go to squeeze my fingers around my switch, I realise they won't move fast enough. I try to squeeze them closed again but they won't obey me. My hand has failed me and a wave of anger pulses through me as I watch the highlighter move on to the next symbol. I have missed fried egg. It has been and gone. I must wait for the cursor to click through the whole grid again before I'll get another chance to select it.

I take a deep breath. Communicating is a particularly arduous game of verbal snakes and ladders for me. It takes the kind of patience I'm now almost glad I had years to master.

I watch as the words light up in front of me once more. Come what may, I will get my fried egg. Then I will click on one last symbol – 'speak' – and my electronic voice will finally have its say.

16

I Tell a Secret

I can't pinpoint the exact moment when I first fell in love with Virna. Perhaps the feeling settled so slowly, layer by layer, that I didn't realise it had become part of me, or maybe I just never allowed myself to think it. But all I know in this moment, as I look at her, is that I love her.

I'm at the day centre and Virna is talking to me. I look forward to her visits now more than ever because they are a soothing antidote to the resentment that's beginning to flicker inside me. I don't understand why I'm still being sent to the care centre even though I'm getting better and better at using my communication system. It's late 2002 – more than a year since I was assessed – and even though I'm sure I've proven I shouldn't be here, no one seems to know what to do with me because there is nowhere else for me to go. If being here was hard when no one knew my intelligence was intact, then it's a thousand times more so now.

I have two lives: one in which I'm at home, working on my

computer, feeling as if I might soon become a part of the world for the first time; and the other, in which I sit in the care home with a folder of symbols lying on my lap that no one takes much notice of, feeling as dead as I ever did. It's getting harder and harder to move between the two.

Not long ago, my parents went away on a short trip and I was sent to an unfamiliar residential home. Each morning I was wheeled into a dirt yard surrounded by a high metal fence, where I would sit like an animal in a zoo. At the end of each afternoon, I was taken back inside, where there was no TV or radio, nothing to break the monotony. The only thing that ever changed was the sound of cars on a nearby road and whenever I heard one approach I dreamed it was someone coming to take me away. But I was never rescued and there was nothing I could do to stem the rage and disappointment surging through my veins. When would people start to see me for who I am instead of the broken shell that encases me? What must I do to convince them that I don't fit into these places any more and it's wrong to try and make me?

Even though some people have seen how much I'm capable of, I'm still usually treated like a child who doesn't know his own mind. It feels as if Virna is the only one who sees me as an equal and I'm more and more certain that I mean something to her. Why else would she have such faith in me? I long ago stopped listening to the staff here making jokes about how much time Virna spends with me. But now I've started to think about what they say and I know her eyes shine with pleasure when she asks how I'm getting on with my computer. I can't tell her a lot about my progress because I don't bring my laptop to the centre for fear something might happen to it.

It is far too precious to bring to this place. But Virna asks me questions that I answer more surely now that my head movements are getting better and my hands a little steadier. Like a rusty old machine that runs more smoothly with use, my body is growing stronger.

But it's not just Virna's interest in my progress that tells me she cares; she's told me in other ways too: by giving me a mobile she'd made of wire fish decorated with sea-green and blue marbles, which now hangs in my bedroom, and by visiting me on my birthday. Virna is the only person who's ever come to see me at home apart from my school friend Stephen, who came around during the years after I fell sick. Each year, he would arrive with a birthday card that he would read out to me. But I've not seen Stephen for a long time now because he moved across the country to study to be a doctor. So I was overwhelmed when Virna came to see me. It happened even before I was assessed and she gave me a box that she'd painted for my birthday. No one but Virna believed in me back then and I gazed at the box in wonder, holding it as gently as a religious relic, as she and her cousin Kim chatted to my parents.

'We'll be back,' Virna said softly as she got up to leave and smiled at me. 'This won't be the last time we visit you.'

That's why I feel so hopeful now that Virna might be able to care for me even more as I learn to communicate. Soon I'll be able to say whatever I want, talk about any subject quickly and easily, and be the kind of person that Virna might like.

I wonder why I'm surprised to realise that I've fallen in love with her. The clues to my feelings were there all along if only I'd looked back long enough to see them. Soon after Virna started working at the centre, I can remember hearing a conversation that should have told me all I needed to know. Envy filled me as I heard her talking to another carer about a cinema date she was going on with a man she'd met. How I longed to be the one to take Virna out and make her smile.

I didn't hear anything more about it until a couple of months later when I heard her talking to Marietta. But this time her eyes didn't dance when she spoke about the man.

'He's not worth getting upset over!' Marietta said to Virna. 'You've just got to forget about him. There are plenty more fish in the sea.'

Virna gave Marietta a weak smile and I could see she was upset. What a fool the man was. She'd felt something real for him and he'd hurt her. It angered me.

I smile to myself now as I think back to that day four years ago when I should have realised I felt something more than just friendship for Virna. Then I look at her as she talks softly to me and I know as certainly as I've ever known anything that I love her.

'My cousin Kim's met a new guy,' she says, her voice bright and excited. 'She really likes him. She wasn't sure what was happening for a while because they went out a few times but he didn't say anything to her about what he wanted.'

I look at Virna. The more I learn about what happens between men and women, the more I realise that what you see on TV isn't like real life: real life is never that simple. But surely this man wouldn't take Kim out if he didn't like her?

'It's all fine now, though,' Virna says with a smile. 'They had a chat last night and he told Kim that he thinks she's great. She's really happy.'

Suddenly, I'm filled with the desire to tell Virna how I feel.

She's told me about Kim and her new boyfriend. I want what they have. I must tell Virna because I'm sure she wants this too.

I lift my hand and watch it wave haphazardly in the air. It flails inconclusively between us but I smile at Virna. I've never told anyone anything like this before, never dared imagine that it might be possible for someone to love me. But surely it is now that I'm learning to communicate and showing people a little of what I'm capable of? Virna, of all people, must be able to see past my broken body?

My hand waves in the air once more before it drops to my side. Virna looks at me silently. Her face is steady and serious. What's wrong with her? She's so quiet.

'Do you think there could be something between us, Martin?' she asks eventually.

I smile, feeling nervous and excited, scared and hopeful. I'm so sure that she feels as I do. Why else would she be a friend like no other? Why else would she help me?

Then I see sadness flicker in Virna's eyes.

'I'm sorry, Martin,' she says.

All the happiness that was rippling off her a few moments ago as she talked to me about Kim has suddenly disappeared. Virna is flat, lifeless. I can feel her withdrawing from me. I want her to stay but she's disappearing.

'We can only ever be friends,' Virna says slowly. 'You must understand that. There never can be anything between us, Martin. I'm sorry.'

My smile sets in my face like concrete. I don't know how to wipe it off as I listen to her speak.

'I'm so sorry if you feel differently,' Virna tells me. 'But I have to be honest and say there will never be anything more between us.'

My smile finally shatters. I can feel a pain in my chest. I've never known anything like it before but I know what it is. I've heard it talked about in movies and listened to people describe it in songs. I understand what it is now even as it pierces me: heartbreak.

17

The Bite

I was sitting on the toilet. I'm not sure why. I must have
been a teenager and maybe Dad had just given me a bath.
Whatever the reason, I was naked and I'd had enough. It had
been a bad day — not bad because something awful had happened but because nothing ever happened.

Dad leaned over and stretched his arms around me. I felt
his fingers closing around a pimple on my back. It hurt. I
didn't want him to touch it. I wanted him to stop, to leave me
alone. I stared at my father's stomach, which was level with
my eyes. It was big, round and sturdy. It wasn't just because
of his beard that my mother often called him 'Father
Christmas'.

Rage welled up inside me as I looked at Dad's stomach. He
leaned even closer and his belly grazed my mouth as I felt his
fingers dig questioningly into my pimple. The pain was so
sharp, I wanted to roar at him to stop, shake his hands off me
and storm out of the room, just as I'd seen Kim and David do

so many times when they were annoyed. For once, I wanted to be able to decide who did what to me, when and how. I wanted my father to stop touching me and just let me be. Even a baby can scream its dissatisfaction but I couldn't even do that.

Rage burned bitter in the back of my throat as I opened my mouth as wide as I could before sinking my teeth into my father's stomach.

He gasped in shock as he stepped back and looked at me in surprise.

'That bloody hurt,' he said as he rubbed his tummy.

Guilt filled me first – and then sweet relief.

18

The Furies

If there were Three Furies in my story, their names were Frustration, Fear and Loneliness. These were the phantoms that plagued me for seven long years – nine if my awareness is dated from the time I started to dip in and out of life. But while the Furies almost beat me many times, thankfully I learned how to defeat them every now and again too.

Frustration came first. If there was an Olympic gold in outrunning her, I'm sure I would have won it. Frustration was a twisted, hissing mistress, unique because she was all-consuming. Fear might have been a sudden cold punch in my stomach and Loneliness a dead weight on my back but Frustration started in my chest, turned my guts into twisted metal and soon overwhelmed my entire body. Every molecule vibrated with anger as she infected me.

Frustration rose up inside me so often because I was constantly reminded that I couldn't determine my own fate in

even the smallest of ways. If people wanted me to sit in the
same position for hour after hour, there was nothing I could
do about it, although pain shot through me. Words can't
express how much I sometimes hated the cold custard and
prunes that I ate every lunchtime for years. And other
people's determination to make me walk was always sure to
start Frustration wailing again.

My parents still believe that I might be able to walk again
because, although they are spastic and uncontrollable, my
limbs aren't paralysed. It was my mother who started taking
me to physiotherapy sessions to make sure my muscles and
joints didn't freeze completely through inactivity. She and my
father were so committed to the belief that I would walk
some day that neither would listen when a doctor suggested
permanently severing some of the tendons in my feet to
reduce the spasticity. He said it wouldn't matter because
surely I would never use my feet again? My parents refused
his advice, took me to see a new medic and two years ago I
had the first of two extensive foot surgeries to flatten my
curled-in feet in the hope that it might help me to walk again
one day.

Not being able to walk always felt almost insignificant to
me compared to my other limitations. It seemed far more
problematic not to be able to use my arms to feed or wash
myself, make a gesture or hug someone. Not having a voice
to say I'd had enough food or the bath water was too hot or
to tell someone I loved them was the thing that made me feel
most inhuman. Words and speech separate us from the animal
kingdom, after all. They give us free will and agency as we use
them to express our desires and refuse or accept what others

want us to do. Without a voice, I couldn't control even the simplest things and that's why Frustration so regularly started her violent lament inside me.

Next came her sister Fear — the fear of being powerless over what happened to me from day to day or in the future, the fear that I was growing up and would be put into permanent residential care because my parents couldn't cope with me as they got older. Every time I was sent to one particular residential home in the country, when my family went on holiday or my father was away on a business trip, terror filled me when I thought I might never leave it again. Those few hours each day with my family were what kept me alive.

I hated that care home in the country more than any other place I was sent. Years ago, after overhearing my parents talk about what time they would leave the next day to take me there, I knew I had to do something to stop them. When Fear woke me up in the middle of the night, I realised I had to rid myself of her forever. After listening to check everyone was asleep, I wriggled my head off my pillow and into the plastic pillowcase encasing it. As it crackled around my head, I pressed my face into the pillow itself as hard as I could as I told myself that I wouldn't have to go to the country the next day; I would soon be free of Fear.

Breathing faster and faster, I began to sweat as my head started to feel light. I'd found a way to escape Fear and I felt elated. But the emotion soon gave way to despair as I realised that I wasn't going to succeed. However hard I tried, I couldn't stop my pitiful body from breathing. The next day I went to the country as planned and carried on visiting the home there once or twice a year.

'They can look after you better than I can,' my mother would tell me again and again if she was the one who was driving me there.

She always said the same thing, like an incantation she hoped would ward off the guilt as it rose inside her.

'You'll be well looked after,' she'd insist, clinging on to the words as she said them.

If Mum had known what happened to me in that place, then I'm sure she never would have said this. But she didn't know and I felt torn between rage and sadness as I listened to her: rage that my parents were making me go to a place I hated so much and sadness that my mother truly seemed to believe strangers could care for me better than she could. The fire of my longing to stay with her burned white hot inside me and I wished she could see it and know how much I wanted to be with her and no one else.

Last came Loneliness and she was perhaps the most terrifying of all the Furies because she could slowly suck the life out of me even as I sat in a room surrounded by people. As they hurried to and fro, chatted, argued, made up and fell out again, I could feel the paralysing bony fingers of Loneliness clamp tightly around my heart.

However isolated she made me feel, Loneliness could always find new ways to make her presence felt. A few years ago I had an anaesthetic after going into hospital for an operation and Mum and Dad had left to go to work by the time I was wheeled into the operating theatre. A nurse held out my arm as a needle was put into a vein and an anaesthetist connected a syringe full of white liquid to it.

'Sweet dreams,' he said softly as I felt a burning sensation move up my arm towards my chest.

The next thing I knew, I was lying on my side on a cold hospital bed. It was moving and I couldn't see properly. I felt utterly disoriented as I struggled to understand where I was. But as I felt a hand take mine to adjust a needle going into a vein, I grabbed on to it as hard as I could, hopeful for a moment of connection that would defeat the feeling of being completely alone. But the hand was pulled roughly from my weak grip and I heard footsteps retreat as I lay squirming with shame, thinking how repulsive I must be.

What saved me was discovering that Loneliness had an Achilles heel, which meant the skein of isolation she wound around me could occasionally be unravelled. I just never knew when it might happen.

I once remember my father talking about a book one of his work colleagues had read. It was about a man who had been disabled as an adult and complained that one of the worst things about sitting in a wheelchair was the discomfort that came from being badly positioned in it. My ears pricked up immediately because as I'd grown older I'd become increasingly aware that I was often left sitting on my balls. The feeling was a very specific type of discomfort: pain gave way to numbness before pain put in a follow-up appearance, like a music hall actress making a bawdily triumphant encore to a delighted crowd.

After the conversation with his colleague, my father was always extra careful to position me gently and make sure I wasn't trapping my testicles beneath me when he sat me in my wheelchair. And each time he did, Loneliness went snarling back to her solitary cave, because when my father showed that he was thinking about me, we defeated Loneliness together.

19

Peacock Feathers

I will my hands not to shake as I stare at the computer. I must think methodically, reason my way step by step through the problem on the screen in front of me. I have to be calm and considered if I'm going to solve it.

'What do you want me to do next?' Virna asks as she sits next to me.

I'm not sure yet. I stare at the screen and feel my mind flipping back through all I've learned about computers, the hours spent watching software demonstrations and practising new programmes. I feel sure the answer is somewhere inside me. I just need to find it.

It's February 2003, a year after I first got my laptop and nearly two years since I was assessed. I'm sitting with Virna in front of a computer at the health centre that shares a building with my care home. She started working here a few months ago and we still see each other often because she is so close by. Virna has remained true to her word that we could be friends even after I told her how I felt, and we talk as we always have. Mostly it's everyday stuff, which is how I knew there were problems with the computers in her office.

'Apparently there are issues with the cooling fans,' she told me.

I doubted if this was the real reason for the glitches. Teaching myself to read might be taking a long time but learning the language of computers has been easy in comparison. Just as I once learned to tell time by memorising shadows, I'm trying to commit letter shapes to memory and can now understand a few written words. Maybe it's simply a question of reawakening the aptitude for electronics I had as a child but I've discovered that I understand computers almost intuitively since getting my own. In recent months I've taught myself to use a string of software programmes, including one that translates my symbols into words so that I can send emails, and another that allows me to answer the phone via my laptop.

'Hello, this is Martin Pistorius speaking,' my computer voice says. 'I am unable to talk so I speak via a computer and this takes some time, so please be patient.'

Even so, most people ring off because the blandness of my computerised voice is so hypnotic they think they're talking to an answerphone. But I have at least started to address the problem after being asked to give a talk about my experiences. The staff here at the health centre had heard my story from people at the care home and asked me to tell them more about my communication system. But after spending forty hours inputting an eight-minute speech, I realised that my voice was so monotonous even Romeo would have bored Juliet if he'd used it to declare his love.

So I started to experiment with ways to make my computer voice sound more natural. First, I inputted full stops into the middle of sentences so that my computer voice would sound as if it was pausing for 'breath'. Next I decided to modify my American 'voice' so that I say 'tomARto' instead of 'tomAYto' in an effort to sound more as I would if I could speak. I also had to choose which voice to use: just as some people pick from a list of fonts when they type, I was able to select one of a dozen voices contained in my computer software. The one I chose is called 'Perfect Paul' because he sounds like a good fit for me – not too high, not too gruff.

Tailoring my speech has certainly made me feel more confident and yet it didn't allay the fear that filled me on the day of the talk itself. I knew I would recognise many of the people in the room and the constant tremor in my hands – one of the legacies of my past – got worse and worse as I became more anxious. Virna was sitting near me while I gave my talk but even so I shook so much I could hardly hit the switches to start the computer. I forced myself to breathe deeply as I stared at the screen and heard my voice start to speak.

'Hello everybody and thank you for coming today,' it said. 'I am really nervous so I wrote a few things down.'

Line by precious line, I went on to describe what had happened to me since the day of my assessment and all that I'd learned since then – the software and symbols, the switches and headmouse – and people came up to congratulate me when I'd finished. Then they turned to discuss what I'd said with each other and it was strange to know they were talking about words I'd spoken. It was the first time that had ever happened.

The ease I have with computers is what made my father suggest I might be able to help with the problems here at the health centre. Apparently he said they should give me a chance to fix them, which is why Virna came to get me from my classroom at the care centre. I think my teacher that day must have thought the world had gone mad if anyone was entertaining the idea that someone from her end of the corridor might be able to fix a computer. But to me it felt like a sign, the chance I'd been waiting for to show what I was capable of.

My nerves twisted as Virna pushed me down the hall. I wanted to prove that I could do more than just speak words via a laptop. Sitting down in front of the computer, I stared at the screen. Virna was going to have to be my hands and use the mouse to navigate into the system so that I could fix it as she read to me what was written on the screen and I told her what to do. Repairing a computer is a bit like going into a maze, after all: you might go down dead ends but eventually you find your way through. I just had to trust my instincts as the computer prompted us with commands and we sat there for hours, fixing first one problem, then another and finally solving a third.

I was filled with exhilaration when we'd finished. I'd done it! I could hardly believe I'd managed to work out a problem that no one else had been able to. I had Virna check the computer again and again just to make sure that I'd really solved it, and each time it was clear the system was working properly again.

'Well done, Martin!' Virna kept saying, smiling at me with pleasure. 'I can't believe you did that. The technicians couldn't manage it but you did!'

She laughed to herself as she pushed me back down the corridor to the care centre. 'That will show them!' she kept saying.

Even going back to my classroom couldn't dampen my mood. I didn't notice where I was any more. I didn't care. All I could see was the computer screen and its inner workings flashing around my head as I navigated myself and Virna around the maze. I'd done it!

A few days later, there was another problem with the email system, and once again Virna told me about it. My heart began to race with excitement and I wished with all my might I'd be asked back to help out again. But it was several days before Virna finally came down the corridor to get me. Maybe her manager thought I'd just been lucky the first time and wasn't sure I'd be able to repeat my success.

But now Virna and I are sitting together in front of a computer screen once more.

'Shall I hit F1?' she asks.

I jerk my head to the side to tell her not to.

'How about F10?'

I smile.

She hits the key and we're taken into the first layer of the computer's modem settings. I know there will be many more to come before I find the problem. I must calm myself down and think clearly. I have to show for a second time what I'm capable of and prove beyond doubt that I really know what I'm doing. I'm focused as I tell Virna where to go next.

Somehow I know I'll be able to fix this problem. I can feel it. I'm sure that with Virna's help I'll be able to navigate my way inside this machine and find whatever is troubling it.

It's then that I feel it – an emotion I hadn't felt until I first fixed the computer last week. Now it's back again and the feeling is strange, like a peacock splaying its multicoloured tail feathers; it puffs me out and makes me feel vital. Then I realise what it is: pride.

20

Daring to Dream

Is there anything more powerful than a mother's love? It's a battering ram that breaks down castle doors, a tidal wave that washes away all in its wake. Mum's eyes are bright with it as she turns to me.

'I'll just run in to check where we need to go and then I'll come back and get you,' she says.

Mum gets out of the car and slams the door. I sit with the spring sunshine pouring through the windscreen, making me squint. We've come to the communication centre where I was first assessed nearly two years ago because I've been invited to attend an open day with students after my mother insisted on updating the experts about my progress.

'You've come so far, Martin!' she told me. 'I'm going to go and see them. They'll want to know. You've only been using your computer for just over a year and look at all you can do on it!'

I knew there was no point trying to stop Mum after she'd

made the decision to boast so I waited while she went off to the centre a few weeks ago and on her return listened while she excitedly told me what had happened.

'They want to see you,' she said. 'They can't believe how quickly you've progressed. They've invited you to attend a workshop with some students.'

I can understand everyone's surprise. Even I feel a little swept off my feet now that I have a job. In fact, I have to check I'm not dreaming each time I'm pushed into the office where I volunteer one day a week. I'm working at the health centre where I helped fix the computers with Virna and I can hardly believe that I'm being asked to do more than stare blankly at the walls of a care home. The work is simple – I photocopy and file because my right arm has grown strong enough to lift paper now and a wonderful colleague called Haseena helps me if there is something I can't do. I also fix the computers as and when problems arise.

The best thing about the job is that it means I've finally been able to leave the care home. It's the strangest feeling every Tuesday when I'm pushed through the doors of the building and my body imperceptibly leans right towards my old classroom, only to be turned in the opposite direction towards the health centre. Leaving the care home is a fork in the road; I'd die if I were sent back to one now. I sometimes wonder whether a shadow of the ghost boy lingers in the place where I spent so many years. But I push the thought away. I refuse to think about the past now that I have a future.

My body is getting stronger in a number of tiny ways as I start to use it more. On the days when I'm not working, I'm at home practising on the computer. I'm a little sturdier when I sit upright now. My neck muscles are strong enough for me to use my headmouse most of the time and I'm beginning to use the touchpad on my laptop a little because my right hand in particular is getting more reliable. My left is still largely uncontrollable so I might not be a butterfly quite yet but I'm slowly emerging from my chrysalis.

The only visible link with my past is the bib I still wear, a legacy of the days when I would drool so uncontrollably down my chest that a speech therapist recommended my mouth be filled with icing sugar to force me to swallow. I don't really need the bib any more and my mother doesn't want me to wear it but I can't quite bring myself to stop. Maybe I'm afraid of losing the magical powers I've gained unexpectedly if I test them too much by taking off the bib. Maybe my reluctance to give up the trappings of my baby years is the only act of rebellion I have at my disposal and I want to make the most of it as I start to realise what it means to make my own decisions. Choosing whether or not to wear my bib each day is often the only opportunity I have to make a decision so I'm determined to be the one to make it.

Now, as I sit inside the car waiting for my mother, I watch students walking up and down the road in front of me. The communication centre is part of a university and I dream of studying at a place like this because I know that one day I'd like to work full-time with computers. There are occasions when they seem like the simplest things in the world compared to everything else I'm learning.

I've even started testing software for a company in the UK. I use their communication programmes on my computer and Mum and I have been finding bugs in the software every now and again since we started using it. The makers used to email solutions to the problems to my mother, but gradually I became the one they corresponded with. When they realised how well I knew the systems, they asked me to start testing them. I've no idea how or why I understand computers so well but I've stopped asking. It's often like that these days: there are things I do without thinking that surprise people.

When my father came into the office recently, he looked at me quizzically as I put documents into alphabetical files.

'How do you know what goes where?' Dad asked in surprise.

I hadn't really thought about it. I still can't read properly but I'd matched the letter I saw on the name of the document to the one on front of the file. Letters are just symbols after all – an 'A' looks like a man clasping his hands above his head, 'M' is the top of a mountain range and 'S' is a slithering snake.

The car door opens and Mum leans down towards me.

'Are you ready?'

She sets my wheelchair beside the door and lifts my legs out of the car before taking my arm in hers. We pull against each other as I stand up before wriggling down into the chair. Mum puts my laptop on my knee and pushes me towards the building, where I watch the electric doors I'd never even seen two years ago glide open to let us in. A woman directs us to a room where coffee is being served and my eyes slide over the people who are standing together and talking. Two of them are men, neither of whom is in a wheelchair, but each carries a box that looks a little like the device Mum and Dad once almost bought me. I look at the men with interest, like an ornithologist might look at a rare bird. I've never met someone as silent as me before.

'Shall we get you ready?' I hear Mum ask.

She pushes me into a small lecture room filled with desks and chairs lined up in neat rows. A woman is unpacking papers as she stands in front of a whiteboard at the other end of the room.

'Where do you want to sit?' Mum asks and I point to the back row of chairs.

When we're settled, Mum unzips my laptop. A peal of notes bursts into life as she switches it on and the woman at the whiteboard looks up. She's middle-aged with cropped grey hair, glasses and a shawl draped around her shoulders. She smiles at me. I look down, unsure what to do. I've never been to something like this before. I haven't sat among a group of people who are learning and discussing things. I don't want them to notice me.

Mum and I wait as people slowly file into the room before sitting down. They chat with each other, say hello and smile until finally everyone is seated and the woman with glasses starts to speak.

'Good morning,' she says with a smile. 'My name is Diane Bryen and I work at Temple University in Philadelphia, where I run a programme called ACES, which aims to help adult users of communication technology determine and govern their own lives.

'I believe this is the way we will help new voices to emerge and break down stereotypes about those with disabilities.'

The woman's voice is bright and full of energy. She looks around the room encouragingly.

'There's no doubt that those with disabilities face significant barriers,' she says. 'Barriers to equal quality education, barriers to getting family support so that children can be raised with that support, barriers to affordable and accessible housing, barriers to equal access to healthcare and employment.

'These are consistent barriers that you come across with each disability group but what I am here to talk about today are not the most obvious injustices. Instead I want to talk about the whole host of other limitations imposed upon people by society because disability is as much about disabling attitudes as it is physical, cognitive or sensory limitations. If someone does not expect or is not expected to achieve, then they never will.'

I look at Dr Bryen. I've never heard someone speak with such passion and conviction about people like me before.

'I believe that if those with disabilities are to break down the barriers facing them then they must realise they have the *right* to, that they can have goals just like anyone else – and to do that they must dare to dream.'

I watch as Dr Bryen looks around the room.

'The man I'd like to meet most before I die is Nelson Mandela,' she says. 'Because despite being imprisoned for so long, he had a dream that he held on to even when he was deprived of freedom and basic nutrition. Mr Mandela was bold in his dream and followed it until he saw it realised.

'I've met other people with dreams too. One of the best bosses I ever had was a man called Bob Williams, who worked in politics and had cerebral palsy. He also had a great job, a service dog and a wife who loved him very much.

'He was living the life he dreamed of and I've met many more people like him. For instance, I know a musician who dreamed of singing and programmed his communication device to do it for him and a lecturer at the university where I work who has cerebral palsy and does a job she loves. Personally, too, I've seen someone I love dare to dream — because my brother is blind.

'Each of these people has achieved so much but what every one of them did was dare to dream. It is a powerful thing and we must all learn to do it.'

Dr Bryen looks at a man sitting near the front of the room.

'What's your dream?' she says to him.

He is able-bodied and shifts uneasily in his seat as the spot-light falls on him.

'To write a book one day,' he says quietly.

'And how are you going to achieve it?'

'I'm not sure.'

Dr Bryen smiles at him.

'That's why we need to think long and hard about our dreams, because once we dare to have them, we can start the process of trying to realise them.

'Dreams don't have to be huge though. I know of one woman who dreams of having a subscription to a soap opera magazine and another who wants to eat macaroni cheese for dinner each week.

'Dreams can be any size you want them to be. But the important thing is that you have one that is yours.'

Dr Bryen looks around the room again. Her eyes travel

over the rows of people, further and further back until they come to rest on me.

'What do you think you need to achieve a dream?' she asks.

Everyone looks at me. I don't know what to say. I want to be left alone. I've never been looked at by so many people at once. I don't know what to do.

'I think Martin would say you need to work hard,' Mum says.

She is speaking for me, trying to fill the silence I'm carving open like a gash. I wish I could disappear.

'But I want to know what *you* think,' Dr Bryen asks as she looks at me. 'It's Martin, isn't it? I want you to tell me what you believe a person needs to achieve their dream.'

There's no escape. The room feels so quiet as I point my headmouse at the laptop and start clicking on switches. After what seems like forever, I finally speak.

'You need to be given the chance to decide for yourself what your dream is,' my computer voice says.

'What do you mean, Martin?'

I click on my switches again and again.

'People must help you work out what your dream is. They must enable you to have one.'

'Oh no!' Dr Bryen exclaims. 'I don't agree with you at all. Don't you see, Martin? You can't ask other people to give you permission to dream. You just have to do it.'

I'm not sure if I understand what Dr Bryen means. I've spent my whole life being given the food others chose for me and put into bed when they decided I was tired. I've been dressed as they saw fit and spoken to as and when they wanted to speak to me. I've never been asked to think about what *I* want. I don't know what it's like to make decisions for myself, let alone dare to dream. I look at her. I know so much about other people's expectations and so little about my own.

But is what she's saying true? Might I really start to make decisions for myself now that I'm finding my voice? I'm only just beginning to realise that somewhere at the end of this journey there might be the kind of freedom I could never even have imagined once. I'll be able to be the person I want to be but do I really dare to dream who he is?

21

Secrets

The unexpected side to being a ghost boy was that people inadvertently showed me their secret worlds. I heard farts rip like bullets from a gun as people walked across a room or watched them check their reflections so often it seemed as if they were hoping to see a more beautiful version of their face magically appear. I've known people to pick their noses and eat what they found or adjust their clinging under-wear before scratching their crotch. I've heard them swear and mumble to themselves as they pace around a room. I've lis-tened to arguments unfold as lies were twisted into facts to try and win a contest.

People revealed themselves in other ways too: in a touch that was gentle and caring or rough and unthinking; in feet that shuffled with fatigue when they walked into a room. If someone was impatient, they would sigh as they washed or fed me; if they were angry, they would pull off my clothes just a little more roughly than usual. Happiness fizzed off them like a small electric pulse, while anxiety had a thousand telltale signs from the nails people bit to the hair they pushed behind their ears again and again to try to contain their worry.

Sadness, though, is probably the hardest thing of all to hide because sorrow has a way of seeping out however well people think they're containing it. You only have to look to see the signs, but most people don't, which is why so many seem to end up feeling lonely. I think that's why some of them talked to me: speaking to another living creature – however inanimate – was better than no one at all.

One of the people who confided in me was Thelma, a carer who worked at the home when I was first there and often ended up sitting with me and some of the other kids as we waited to be picked up at the end of the day. Every afternoon, I would sit listening for the white gate at the end of the corridor to squeak open as someone pushed it. Then, as footsteps started to echo down the hall, I'd try to work out who it was: the click of high heels meant that Corinne's mum had come to get her, heavy army boots told me it was Jorika's father, while the soft pad of Dad's shoes spoke of the sturdy man he still is today and my mother's shoes were almost silent except for the muffled rustle of her rapid steps. Some days I could guess who everyone was before I saw them but on others I got them all wrong.

Each afternoon the other children would leave one by one and the building would slowly fall silent: phones would stop ringing and people would stop rustling, my ears would hiss as the air conditioning was switched off and my brain would fill the silence with white noise. Soon it would be just Thelma and me waiting and I was always glad it was her because she didn't get angry if my father was late.

One afternoon we were sitting together when a song came on the radio and Thelma stared into space as she listened to it. I could feel she was sad today.

'I miss him so much,' she said suddenly. Although my head was bent to my chest, I could hear that she had started to cry.

I knew what she was talking about: her husband had died. I'd heard people speaking about it in low voices.

'He was a good man,' she whispered. 'I think of him all the time, every day.'

There was a creak as Thelma shifted her weight on the chair beside me. Her voice cracked as she spoke and her tears fell faster.

'I can't stop seeing him at the end. I keep wondering if he understood what was happening. How did he feel? Was he scared or in pain? Did I do enough? I keep going over and over it in my mind. I can't stop thinking of him.'

She sobbed even more.

'If only I'd told him more that I loved him,' she said. 'I didn't say it enough and now I won't get a chance again. I'll never be able to tell him.'

Thelma cried a little more as I sat beside her. I could feel my stomach knotting inside me. She was a kind person who didn't deserve such sadness. I wished I could tell her she'd been a good wife – I was sure she had been.

22

Out of the Cocoon

Was it inevitable that I would become terrified of solitude after spending so many years alone? After attending the workshop at the communication centre last month, I'm back attending a week-long course about augmentative and alternative communication or AAC. Everyone, from people like me who use AAC to the parents, teachers and therapists working with us, comes to this centre. But this particular course is for students studying for a degree in AAC, and I was invited to take part by the centre's director, Professor Alant. Mum has come with me each day but this morning she has had to go to a hardware shop because there's a problem with one of my switches. It means I'm all alone.

As I look around the room full of strangers, I realise that I can't remember ever being without a family member or carer close by. I spent years in enforced solitary confinement inside myself but I was never physically alone until now. I can't remember being a child who ventured further and further down the road until I found the courage to turn the corner alone for the first time. I was never a teenager who took my first steps towards adulthood and independence as I defied my parents by staying out all night.

I feel terrified. What should I say? What should I do? I sit in my chair at the back of the lecture room, hoping to be inconspicuous, and breathe a sigh of relief when the first lecture starts. Then there's the tea break. I know that if I'm going to join in someone will have to push my chair for me, put a straw into a mug and put it near enough for me to bend my head down to drink it. So when one of the students asks if I'm coming for tea, I tell her that I would prefer to stay where I am. I'm too scared to accept the offer. I don't want to be a burden or impose myself on people I don't know.

But as I sit in the room and watch people file out past me, chatting and laughing together, I know that my resistance is pointless. I will always need help to navigate through the so-called real world – to move around, negotiate doors, eat, drink and go to the toilet. I can't do any of these things alone so if a stranger wants to open a door, I must smile at them; if someone offers to push me up a step, I have to accept their help even if I don't want it. It's only when I begin to let strangers help me that I'll start moving beyond the limiting place where my parents are always with me and everyone is familiar. As the cocoon I've been hidden in for so long begins to break apart, I have to learn new ways.

'Martin?'

I look up to see Michal, a speech therapist at the communication centre I'd met at the workshop last month.

'Shall I take you to the tea room and we'll get a drink?' she asks.

Michal smiles. Relief floods into me. I click on just one symbol.

'Thank you.'

23

An Offer I Can't Refuse

Apparently I'm a rare species. Like a parrot or a monkey, I'm of interest to the experts. Partly it's because I'm both a new user of AAC and a young adult, which is somewhat unusual. Most people who learn to communicate via AAC are either children who have been born with problems like cerebral palsy, autism or a genetic disorder, or older adults who have lost their speech through illnesses such as strokes or motor neurone disease. People like me, who lose their speech in the middle of life rather than at the beginning or end through illness or accident, are rarer. But more important is the fact that I've learned so much so quickly about computer communication *and* I'm teaching myself to read and write — that's the real novelty because many AAC users never become literate. So the students have gathered to listen to me speak on the last day of the course.

'Adjusting to my new life has been challenging and frightening at times,' I tell them. 'There's so much I don't know and

I've often felt completely overwhelmed. I'm on a steep learning curve but everything is changing drastically for the better.'

As the students swarm around to congratulate me after my speech, I feel uplifted to be among them. People my own age seem so bright, as if they've been drawn in rainbow colours, with their huge smiles and loud voices. In honour of the occasion, I decided to stop wearing my bib and I look a little more like them now.

'You were great!' I hear an American voice say.

Erica is a student I met earlier this week on the morning when Mum had gone to the store and Michal took me for tea. After getting me a drink, Michal got distracted and I stared at my cup, knowing I wouldn't be able to drink what was in it because she hadn't given me a straw.

'Do you need something?' a voice asked.

I turned my head to see a woman who looked to be about my age. She had short blonde hair and energy bubbled off her. I waved my hand downwards.

'It's in your bag?'

The woman bent down, found a straw and put it into my mug.

'My name's Erica,' she said. 'Do you mind if I join you?'

I liked how direct she was. Erica told me she was on a ten-month visit from her university in America, where she had studied to be a speech and language therapist; now she was doing a postgraduate course in South Africa. I marvelled at how she talked to me about anything and everything. It wasn't often that someone spoke to me so easily.

'I don't find it cold here even though it's the middle of winter!' Erica said with a giggle. 'I'm so used to harsh winters in Wisconsin that this is nothing. I can't believe everyone looks so cold when all I want is to walk around in a T-shirt.'

We carried on chatting until the tea break was over and Erica pushed me back to the lecture room.

'It's been nice talking to you, Martin,' she said.

We've chatted on and off ever since and now Erica is smiling at me once again. She looks mischievous as she bends down towards me.

'I've decided that we should be friends,' she says.

She leans closer so that no one else can hear.

'But there's one condition: no parents.'

I smile at Erica as I give her my email address and she heads off to talk to someone else as Professor Alant comes to see me.

'I'd like to talk to you if possible, Martin?' she says. 'Alone, if that's okay?'

I'm sure that I must look almost as surprised as my mother does. I don't often talk one on one with people I don't know. But Professor Alant looks resolute as she sits down beside me and my mother leaves us.

'We've enjoyed having you with us this week,' she says. 'Have you enjoyed being here?'

I nod.

'I'm glad because your insight into being an AAC user is invaluable and we've been so impressed by all the hard work you've put in and the amazing results you've achieved,' she tells me. 'That's why I want to speak to you, because your mother has told me you're doing voluntary office work one day a week and apparently you enjoy it a lot.

'So I wanted to ask if you'd consider doing a work trial

here too? I'd like to see how it goes one morning a week for the next month and then we can discuss the possibility of something more permanent. How does that sound?'

I stare at Professor Alant in disbelief. I'm too surprised to look at my laptop, let alone programme it with a reply. My world isn't just opening up – it's exploding.

24

A Leap Forward

'What do you think, Martin?'

Juan looks at me expectantly. She works here at the communication centre and is one of my new colleagues.

I'm not sure what to say. Juan wants to know what I think would best help a child who was assessed here recently. But I'm so unused to being asked my opinion that I don't know how to give it properly yet. Working here is so different to the health centre, where many people seemed unsure at first about how to interact with someone like me.

'Can you find the January files, please?' they might ask Haseena, my colleague, when they walked into our office.

Even if she was obviously busy, there were those who didn't ask me to help them. It took time for people to trust me professionally and I enjoy the fact that they do now.

But here, at the communication centre, people have asked me what I think from the moment I arrived. I'm the one person who has put their theories into practice and they're keen to know my opinion. This unnerved me at first but I'm slowly getting used to it.

The first day I came to work here, I sat in the same room where Shakila had once assessed me and I realised I had even less of an idea about what was expected of me now. I was going to have to make my own decisions about how to start and finish the admin tasks I'd been given, such as creating a story written in symbols for the centre's newsletter.

In the second week, I was moved into an office with a woman called Maureen, whom I soon became friends with, and by the third week I'd discovered how invigorating it was to be in a place where people weren't afraid of me.

It's now the fourth week I've been at work and this morning is the end of my trial – the moment of truth. To calm my nerves about my upcoming meeting with Professor Alant, Erica pushes me through the campus to get a coffee. We've become good friends. It's a beautiful spring morning. The trees are heavy with blossom and the sky is bright blue above us.

'Do you think you'll get the job?' Erica asks.

On my lap lies a large laminated sheet covered in the letters of the alphabet. It also contains commonly used words and phrases like 'Thank you' and 'I want'. I use this alphabet board a lot now that I'm spelling better because it's not always practical to have a laptop with me. Literacy is an inexact science though. While I still find reading hard, writing is easier for some reason; I'm not sure why. Maybe it's because writing means breaking down words into their individual letter shapes rather than reading a whole string of symbols that have blurred together to make a word.

'I hope so,' I tell Erica as I point to the letters in front of me. 'I really do.'

'I think you will.'

'How come?'

'Because you're brilliant, Martin!'

I am not so sure. Being in an office has revealed to me just how huge the gaps in my knowledge are. With no memories of my formal education, my brain is a dumping ground where bits of information are thrown together and I have no idea where they come from. In many ways, I feel further behind now than I did before.

Mum and Dad are waiting as Erica and I arrive at the centre and then the three of us go in to see Professor Alant.

'I have to be honest and say that situations like this often don't work out,' she says as soon as my parents sit down.

My heart sinks.

'But even so, we would like to offer you a paid position here, Martin,' Professor Alant says with a smile. 'We feel you could provide really invaluable assistance to the work we do and we'd like you to become a salaried member of staff working one day a week. How does that sound?'

'That's great news!' my father exclaims.

He smiles broadly at me and my mother beams too.

'There are conditions to this offer, though, because if you are to become a member of staff, you will need to be as independent as possible,' Professor Alant adds. 'We'll do all we can to help you achieve this but the one thing you need that we can't provide is an electric wheelchair you can operate independently.

'At the moment, your wheelchair needs to be pushed by

someone but that won't always be possible when you're work-ing alongside colleagues.'

I nod as Professor Alant speaks.

'The reason I'm saying this, Martin, is because your job here won't work if you have to rely on the other staff to help you.'

I look at my parents, praying they will agree to this.

'We understand,' my mother says. 'I'm sure Martin will be only too pleased to do everything he can to help. This job means a great deal to him.'

I nod.

'There's just one other thing,' Professor Alant says. 'I think you need to consider projecting a more professional image and I'd suggest perhaps a shirt and trousers?'

I stare down at my familiar T-shirt and jogging bottoms. My mother opens and closes her mouth like a goldfish.

'Does that sound acceptable?' Professor Alant asks.

My finger points to one word on my alphabet board.

'Yes,' I reply.

'Then that's all agreed,' she says with a smile. 'Welcome to the team, Martin. I'll look forward to seeing you next week.'

My father pushes me out into the hall but no one speaks until we're safely out of earshot.

'Your clothes?' my mother exclaims incredulously. 'What's wrong with your clothes?'

She sounds a little angry. Mum has always bought my clothes and I've never given them any thought.

'And did you hear what she said about things like this never working out?' Mum continues. 'What did she mean?'

'I think she was just trying to say that employing someone with a disability can be challenging,' my father says softly.

'Well then, she hasn't met anyone like Martin before, has she?' my mother roars. 'If anyone can do it, he can. You'll show them, won't you?'

My parents look down at me as we reach the front door of the centre. It is almost two years to the day since our first visit here for my assessment.

'Well, we'll leave you to get on with your day,' Dad says as he squeezes my shoulder, his grip tightening as he wordlessly expresses his excitement.

'You'll prove anyone who doubts you wrong, won't you, son?' Mum says as she smiles. 'I know you will.'

Happiness bursts inside me as I look at them. I hope I will make them proud.

25

Standing in the Sea

I had only the rarest glimpses of my father's feelings when I was the ghost boy. Once, as he came into the lounge after everyone else had gone to bed, I felt hopelessness seep from him in the darkness.

'Martin?' he said as he looked at me.

I was silent, of course, as Dad sat down in a chair and began to talk. As he sat staring out of the window at the night beyond, he told me about his childhood in the country. When he was growing up, my grandfather, GD, always wanted to be a farmer but he ended up working in the mines. Even so, he tried to provide as much as possible for his family by growing food like potatoes, peas and onions and harvesting honey from his beehives. He also had cows to provide milk, cream and butter and one of these animals had provoked my father into a childish act of vicious rebellion he'd never forgotten. Now he told me about it in the silence of the night.

'I hit one of the cows with a stick,' Dad said softly. 'I can't remember why I did it any more but I cut its eyelid. I should never have done it.'

He was silent for a moment.

'But for some reason I can't stop thinking about it now and I think it's because when I remember that day, I realise I got more reaction from a cow than I get from you, my own son.

'I just don't understand how that can be. How can you be so still and silent year after year?'

Dad's breath came out of him in jagged gulps. I longed to comfort him, but there was nothing I could do as he sat silently until his breathing evened out again. Then he stood up and bent down to kiss me on the forehead as I felt his hands close softly around my head. He held it for a few seconds just as he did every night.

'Let's get you to bed, boy,' he said.

That was the only time during all the years he cared for me alone that my father ever gave me any hint of just how desperate he felt at times. But I didn't realise how much his unwavering strength had sustained me until I went on holiday with my family for the first time when I was twenty-five.

Usually I went into residential care when they went away but this time I was taken on the trip to the sea. I was so excited. I couldn't remember seeing the sea before and the huge rolling mass took my breath away. I did not know whether to be awed or afraid. The sea repelled me as much as it fascinated me. Over the years, I'd learned to like the way water lifted and supported my body, freed me in a way that nothing else could. But I'd always found it frightening to think I had no defences against it and wouldn't be able to kick my legs or paddle my arms enough to keep above the surface if I started to sink.

I felt both excited and scared as my father pushed my wheelchair closer to the waterline and I listened to the beat of the waves. Then he helped me to my feet and started shuffling me across the sand towards the water. But the closer I got to it, the more fearful I became and my father must have felt it.

'Relax, Martin,' Dad kept saying again and again as the waves began to curl over my feet.

But I couldn't listen. Adrenalin pumped through my body and my powerlessness felt more overwhelming than ever before as I confronted the sea. I knew it could take me so easily if it wanted to.

My father guided a few more of my halting steps into the water.

'You're safe,' he kept telling me.

But I felt terrified as the sea closed around my feet and legs. I was sure I was going to be swept away and I'd have no choice but to go. Suddenly I felt Dad lean closer to me.

'Do you really think that I would let you go?' he shouted above the sound of the waves. 'Do you think that after all these years, I would let something happen to you now?

'I'm here, Martin. I've got you. I won't let anything happen. There's no need to be scared.'

And it was only in that moment, as I felt my father's arms holding me upright and his strength keeping me steady, that I knew his love was strong enough to protect me from an ocean.

26

She Returns

I open my eyes in the darkness. My heart thumps. Terror fills me. I want to scream, yell, cry out the fear that is running cold in my veins.

I turn my head to look at the clock.

It's 5 a.m., the fourth time I've woken tonight, and just 47 minutes since I last opened my eyes to try and escape my dreams. Tonight they are particularly bad. I wonder if they will ever stop. These are the moments when I feel most alone, as the world sleeps peacefully and I wake in the grey light of an empty dawn.

The nightmare that woke me this time was not so very different from the last. They never are. If my dreams weren't so terrifying, they would be almost boringly predictable.

She was standing in front of me, looking down at my face. I knew what she was going to do and I wanted to push her away, but I couldn't. My arms stayed beside me as lifeless as

.ever as her face came closer. I felt horror surge up my throat as I longed to plea for mercy.

Then I woke up.

It's like this most nights now. However hard I try to submerge the past, it bubbles up into the cracks I can't fill with thoughts of work and home, lists of jobs to do and things I want to experience.

What exhausts me is that I'm no longer haunted only at night. On any ordinary day a thousand tiny triggers lie in wait for me; these are things that no one else would notice but they instantly take me back to the past: a few lilting notes of classical music play in a shopping centre and I'm back at the home in the country where I was trapped like an animal and longed for escape.

'It's so peaceful here,' my mother always used to say when she dropped me off for a stay.

As we entered the building, the restful tones of Vivaldi or Mozart were usually seeping out of a stereo somewhere and I would look at my mother, pleading for her to understand what the music was hiding.

That's why hearing it sends me hurtling back to the past. Or I see a car that reminds me of the one driven by a person who used to hurt me and I'm there again: heart beating, sweat pricking cold across my skin and breath coming in gasps.

No one seems to notice when this happens. Have I really learned to disguise my feelings so well that I can hide even such raw terror from view? I don't understand how I do it but somehow I can. I'm completely alone as I try to bring myself back to the present by reminding myself that the past is behind me.

My heart begins to still as I lie in bed. I must fall asleep again, however fearful I am of being sent back to the world I try so hard to forget. I want to be bright and alert tomorrow at work. I can't let what happened once ruin this chance for me. I can't let it pull me down.

I close my eyes but still I see her face.

27

The Party

The girl sways as she stands in front of me. Her eyes look dazed and she's smiling.

'You're handsome,' she says. 'I'm going to flirt with you.'

Music pumps out of a stereo. The beat is like a hammer and the room is full of students I don't know. I'm at a party on the university campus with Erica and other friends called David and Yvette I met through her.

I can't quite believe I'm here. The theme of the party is 'jungle' and I'm dressed as the king of it with banana leaves in a crown on my head. I've even tried alcohol for the first time after so many people asked me if I wanted anything to drink that I asked Erica to get me a rum and Coke.

'What do you think?' she asked with a smile as I took a sip.

The alcohol filled my mouth before tickling my nose. It was strong and pungent. I didn't like the taste. I smiled half-heartedly at Erica, who was wearing a sarong and had her fluffy toy monkey Maurice hanging around her neck. I leaned my head forward to finish my drink. I wanted to get the odd-tasting concoction out of the way as soon as possible.

'Sip it!' Erica shrieked before laughing.

I took another gulp of the drink and swallowed it quickly.

'Why don't I get you a straight Coke?' Erica asked.

I smiled at her before she disappeared into the crowd and I wondered if she'd find her way back to me or whether anyone else would talk to me. My alphabet board was lying on my lap ready to chat but I wasn't sure anyone would see me sitting down because the room was so crowded. Then the girl who is standing over me now found me.

'What star sign are you?' she asks as she leans towards me.

She is wearing a gold dress and butterfly wings on her head. She has dark hair and a mouth full of huge white teeth. She is pretty and has nice eyes.

'K-A-P-P-R-Y-K-O-R-N,' I spell out on my board.

'Crappy?'

'K-A-P-P-R-Y-K . . .'

'Oh! Do you mean Capricorn?'

I nod. My spelling is still very bad. People have to think laterally if they want to talk to me.

'That's no good,' the girl says. 'I'm Libra.'

What does she mean? I look at the girl as I wonder what to say. She is drunk. Why is she talking to me about astrology? Is this just the white noise that I'm supposed to fill before asking her out on a date? I know nothing about how men and women behave with each other. All I've seen is what's on the TV or in stolen moments of other people's lives. But slowly

I'm discovering that talking to women in any other way than as friends is like using a language I hardly know exists, let alone speak. Is this one in front of me now flirting, as she promised she would?

I have the words at my disposal to talk to women, of course, the lingual mechanics of sex and relationships that Mum and I inputted onto my word grids. It was inevitable we would get to a topic that is just a short step from words like hug and kiss. And even though my mother was the one who had to give the new vocabulary to me, I knew I wanted to have it because sex intrigues me as much as it does any twenty-something man. People might think someone like me has been neutered but they'd be wrong.

In the early days of my awareness, I would count down the time until a French TV drama was shown at the weekend because I knew I'd see women wearing corsets so tight their breasts spilled out of them. Seeing them made me aware of feelings I'd never had before and I enjoyed them. My sexual awareness then told me I wasn't completely dead. It's something I've thought about more since learning to communicate, as I begin to hope that one day a woman might want to be with me.

'Where shall we start?' Mum said in her most resolute voice as we sat together to build the new grid of words. 'Erection?'

At least she didn't have to explain that one. I had them like everyone else.

'Vagina.'

No need for a description of that either. I'd picked up most words on this subject along the way.

But I could have sworn Mum's voice was getting louder and I prayed that David wouldn't hear what we were doing.

'Orgasm!' Mum exclaimed.

'Ejaculation.'

'Sperm.'

My face turned crimson as I waved my hand to plead with my mother to stop.

'No, Martin!' she said. 'You need to know all this. It's important.'

Time stood still as my mother carried on intoning words from the sexual vocabulary. With each second that passed, I wished harder than ever that she'd stop, even as I railed against being a suddenly unwitting hostage to her desire to ensure I was fully informed. It was only when Mum had finally decided enough was enough that I could ask her to hide the grid deep within the others, somewhere only I could find it.

I'd suspected then that I might not use it that much and now I know I won't as I look at the girl standing in front of me. The words I have are too cold and clinical. Talking to women seems to be more about understanding the gaps between the words than the words themselves, interpreting the silent nuances that mean so much. But I have no idea how to do it. I know nothing. Does this girl expect to be kissed by me? And if she does, what do I do? Does she want me to reach out for her or sit waiting until she kisses me? And if she does, then how do I kiss? I've never kissed anyone before. The list of questions in my brain gets longer and longer until it almost seizes up, just as a computer crashes when too much is asked of it.

'Do you know that Capricorns and Librans are incompatible?' the girl asks suddenly.

I really don't understand what she's talking about. I decide to change the topic.

'What course are you doing?' I spell out on my alphabet board.

'Economics.'

I'm not sure what economists look like but I don't think they usually wear butterfly wings on their head. I'm silent as I wonder what to say and the girl weaves around in front of me.

'I'm going to talk to my friends,' she says suddenly. 'Bye.'

She lurches off across the room and I'm left alone again. Will I ever understand? My eyes scan the room as I look at men and women dancing and chatting, laughing at each other's jokes and leaning closer towards each other. One couple is kissing and another man has his arm around a girl's shoulders. I wonder if I'll ever learn the code that will gain me entry to their world.

'Are you okay?'

It's Erica. At least things are simple with her because we both know there's nothing more than friendship between us. Erica has a special place in my heart because over the past three months she has shown me so much of what the world has to offer.

Before we met, my parents did things with me like taking me shopping and to the cinema. I knew I would never forget the first moment in that twilight world when people stared upwards as music started to play and faces the size of skyscrapers rose on the screen above me. I could hardly believe it was real. Why then did everyone around me look almost expressionless? I could see neither fascination nor delight on their faces and I wondered if it was possible to get so used to joy that you stopped noticing it?

But with Erica I've seen how people my own age live. I've experienced the fun of eating hamburgers in McDonald's, wasting an afternoon wandering through a shopping centre and tasting biscuits that she's just baked in the oven. We've also visited botanical gardens and an orphanage, where we cuddled abandoned babies who would die without the kindness of a human touch. I understand that feeling well.

All of it amazes me and Erica seems to enjoy showing me. She's a special person – the first I've encountered, apart from my family and those paid to care for me, to accept my physical limitations without question. With Erica, I know they are only part of what defines me rather than the whole, and she treats me as she would any other friend. She's never said a word or given me a glance that has made me feel like a burden she's embarrassed to carry. Even when I've stayed over at her flat and she has had to lift me on and off the toilet or get me dressed, she's done it easily. Care that's given in spite of someone's distaste is easily recognisable but with Erica it's not an issue. Perhaps that's why I can sleep for hours on end when I stay at her flat, free of my nightmares for one precious night.

'Are you ready to go?' Erica asks.

We leave the party with David and Yvette and cross the road to Erica's. When we get to the flight of stairs leading to the flat, David and Erica stand me up out of my wheelchair and support my weight as I slowly shuffle up the stairs step by step. I smile as I listen to the others talk about who did what, where and with whom. I wish I understood what it all meant.

'I'm sorry if that wasn't the best first party,' Erica says when we get into her flat. 'The music was awful, wasn't it?'

I have no idea but the party was unforgettable.

28

Henk and Arrietta

Love between men and women has always interested me: the way it ebbs and flows like a living thing, or how it is revealed in secret smiles or anguished conversations. Perhaps I've always found it so captivating because it was the starkest reminder of how alone I was.

The first time I saw love was soon after I became aware again. At that time a woman called Arrietta was working part time at my care centre and her son, Herman, was a pupil there. Arrietta had a daughter called Anya, who must have been about three, and on this particular day she was with us at the care centre as we waited for my father to come. I knew Arrietta's husband, Henk, would soon arrive to take his family home, just as I knew my stomach would thrill when he did because I'd be able to see the gun he always carried on his hip. Henk was a policeman and however many times I saw the gun I couldn't believe I was lucky enough to see a real one up close.

Henk knew Arrietta would have to stay until I was collected when he saw me lying on a mat on the floor. I watched
him kiss Arrietta before sitting down at the table to wait and
opening his newspaper, just as he always did. Herman
and Anya were playing outside on the veranda. As Arrietta
walked out into the sunlight to check on them, I watched the
contours of her breasts appear through the thin fabric of her
blouse.

'Did you have a good day?' Henk asked Arrietta as she
walked back inside.

'Long,' she replied as she started to pack up some toys.

They were silent for a minute.

'We need to stop at the supermarket on the way home,'
Arrietta said absent-mindedly. 'What would you like to eat?'

Henk looked at Arrietta.

'You,' he replied, his voice a little deeper than usual.

How could Henk eat Arrietta? I didn't understand what he
meant. She stopped what she was doing to look at him as she
laughed softly.

'We'll have to see about that,' she said.

Suddenly it felt as if time had stopped as Henk and
Arrietta smiled at each other. I knew I was seeing something
new: the secret world of adults that I'd begun to suspect
existed as I grew older. Just as my body was changing and
chairs I'd used for years had slowly became too small for me
even as I began to be shaved regularly, I had caught glimpses
of things between adults that I'd not seen before. They
intrigued me.

Now there was something about Henk and Arrietta's
voices, the softness in them and the smile they shared. I didn't

understand what it was but the air between them hummed for those brief moments, as Henk looked at his wife and she smiled. Then they looked away from each other and the moment was gone.

'Tell me about them,' Henk said to Arrietta as he gestured at the empty room.

They were back to their ordinary selves just as quickly as they'd gone to a place I didn't recognise.

'Who?'

'The children here – I come every day and don't know anything about them.'

Arrietta sat down next to Henk as she started telling him about some of the children I knew so well: Robby, who'd been injured when his father's car crashed into the back of a coal truck and now cried for hours each day. Katie, who was born with a degenerative syndrome and loved food so much that she'd been nicknamed 'Little Fatty'; Jennifer, who'd been born with a brain the size of a chicken's egg after her mother fell ill during pregnancy and shrieked with joy every time she saw her father at the end of each day; Elmo, Jurike, Thabo and Tiaan; Doorsie, Joseph, Jackie and Nadine, who each had a story to tell. Then there were the children who came and went so quickly I never learned their names, like the little girl who was born with learning difficulties and raped by an uncle whose final act of cruelty was to set fire to her genitals.

'What about him?' Henk said finally as he gestured to me.

'Martin?'

'Yes.'

Arrietta told him my story and Henk listened silently until she'd finished.

'His is the saddest,' he said as he looked at me.

'Why?'

'Because he wasn't born like that. He was healthy and then his parents had to watch their child suffer without knowing why. I don't know if I could bear it.'

Arrietta put her arm around him as they looked at me.

'None of us knows what we can bear until we're asked,' she told him gently.

29

The Healer

After seeing Henk and Arrietta's secret world, I was on the lookout for love as I discovered that what I'd seen was rare. It was something unlike anything I'd ever known, and I hoped to get another glimpse of it. Although I had to wait, eventually I saw love again when I was about nineteen.

It happened after my father had a work meeting with a man he didn't know and the stranger turned to Dad as they ate lunch together afterwards.

'How is your son?' he asked.

'Which one?' my father replied in surprise.

'The one who's dying,' the man said.

A rush of anger filled Dad at being asked about the most private part of his family history. But something about the man piqued his interest and that night I heard him telling my mother about their conversation.

'He wants to see Martin,' Dad said as I listened. 'He's a faith healer and believes he can treat him.'

My mother had no reason not to allow it because she'd accepted long ago that the answer to the mystery of my illness would never be provided by traditional medicine. So a few weeks later Dad took me to a flat in the suburbs, where a short, grey-haired man with a beard was waiting for us.

He told me his name was Dave and I knew at once he was kind: his eyes were full of light as he looked at me. I was lifted out of my wheelchair and laid on a bed. Then Dave fell completely silent as he closed his eyes and placed his hands a few centimetres above my chest. He started moving them up and down my body, following the contours of my withered frame but never making contact with it. I felt my skin prickling with waves of heat.

'Your son's aura has been fractured,' Dave eventually said to Dad. 'It's rare but it happens when something traumatic has occurred.'

Dave fell silent again and spoke only once more during the next hour to tell my father that he thought I had problems with my stomach because he could feel pain there. I didn't understand how he knew what none of the doctors did and it scared me. But Dave didn't say any more as he fell silent again and carried on working.

'Can I pay you for your time?' my father asked when Dave had finally finished.

'No,' he replied. He never once asked my parents for a penny although he continued to see me every week for the next three years. It was as if Dave had a calling to treat me, a belief so strong that he had to act.

Each time I saw him, a look of complete concentration would come over his face as he tried to open up the deep reservoir of self-healing energy he believed my body held. Running his hands over the air just above it, he would map the aura he said he could feel had been damaged by my illness. His face still, peaceful and relaxed, his eyes always closed, he concentrated on healing me. Then, when the treatment was over, his features would become as animated as ever.

Months turned into years and as far as the people around me knew, there had been no improvement in my condition. But Dave's faith didn't waver. He still saw me week in, week out, and bent to hold his hands above me with the most intense look of peace and concentration I'd ever seen.

Gradually I began to look forward to seeing him more and more, because as time passed he started talking to me a lot, laughing and joking with me, telling stories about lions and animals that I wished he would write down in books for children one day. His words came in a soothing stream of smiles and jokes as I was laid on the bed and he worked to cure me.

It was about two years after I first met Dave that he married a fellow healer called Ingrid and the two of them started to treat me together from time to time. One morning, as I lay looking up at them, they abruptly stopped what they were doing as they gazed at each other and suddenly the world stopped just as it had when Henk and Arrietta looked at each other. There was no reason why Dave and Ingrid had stopped, no sign that it was going to happen. But just as a ball hangs in the air a moment too long before plummeting towards the ground, time slowed down. Emotion crackled between Dave and Ingrid as their eyes locked and they leaned forward to kiss each other.

'I love you,' they murmured before smiling.

I knew I'd seen that secret world again and wished I understood it. I didn't know what happened between two people. It seemed so strange and mysterious, like an alchemy that willed something into existence. But even though that was the only time I saw it happen between Dave and Ingrid; I knew afterwards it was always there.

One weekend about six months later Dad and I pulled into Dave's driveway to see an unfamiliar car parked there. A Mercedes.

'Have you got lucky, Dave?' Dad asked with a smile as he got me out of the car.

'No!' Dave replied. 'It's my boss's car. He was going away for the weekend with his wife so I drove them to the airport and I'm picking them up tomorrow.'

He and my father began to chat about events a world away as I was pushed inside.

'Have you seen the pictures on TV?' Dave asked my father. 'It's extraordinary.'

I knew what they were talking about. Princess Diana had been killed in a car crash and the outpouring of emotion that had followed her death had been all over South African television screens. I'd watched the footage of flowers piled high in an English palace garden and thought about them now – such an outpouring of love for one woman, a person who had touched so many lives.

After Dave finished treating me, he said he would see me again the next week and then said goodbye. But two days later, Kim came to pick me up from the care centre and we got home to find our parents waiting. I knew instantly that something terrible had happened.

'Dave is dead,' my father said to Kim in a rush as she helped me out of the car.

I felt a pain in my chest as I listened to my parents tell Kim what had happened. The previous night, Dave and Ingrid had got into the Mercedes to drive to the airport to pick up Dave's boss and his wife just as they'd promised. But as they'd reversed out of their gate, some men had jumped in front of them and demanded the car. In the beam of the headlights, Dave and Ingrid could see the men had guns.

The robbers also wanted their jewellery and Dave had silently handed them his watch and wedding ring, hoping it might be enough to persuade them to go. But suddenly, without warning, one of the men pulled the trigger and a single shot went through Dave's forehead. As he slumped forward, another car pulled up, which the robbers jumped into. Dave survived for just a few hours after being airlifted to hospital and the robbers were never caught.

'It's so terrible,' my mother said sadly. 'How could they do it? He was such a good man.'

I felt breathless as I heard the news, unable to believe Dave's life had been ended so brutally. I thought how unfair it was that I'd clung on to mine even when I hadn't wanted it at times and yet Dave, who had loved his so much, had lost it. Then I thought of Ingrid and the love that had been extinguished by a bullet. I still didn't fully understand what I'd seen between her and Dave so many months before but instinctively I knew her grief for its loss would be almost unbearable.

30

Escaping the Cage

Learning to communicate is like travelling along a road only to find the bridge you need to cross the river has been washed away. Even though I have thousands of words on my grids now, there are still ones I think of but don't have. And when I do have them, how do I take a thought and put it into symbols or feel an emotion and trap it on a screen? Talking is about so much more than words and I'm finding the ebb and flow, rhythm and dance of it almost impossible to master.

Just think of the man who raises his eyebrows when the waiter gives him the restaurant bill for the anniversary dinner he's just had with his wife.

'You've got to be joking!' he says as he looks at it.

As his wife listens, she'll know from his tone and look whether his words are an angry accusation about money he begrudges or an affectionate ribbing of the woman he would spend his last penny on. But I can't spit out syllables in anger or shriek them happily; my words will never quaver with emotion, rise expectantly for a laugh just before a punchline or drop dangerously in anger. Instead I deadpan each and every one electronically.

After tone, comes space. I used to spend hours day-dreaming about what I'd say or having endless conversations in my head. But now that I'm able to talk, I don't always get the chance to say what I want to. A conversation with me is slow and takes time and a patience that many people don't have. The person I talk to must sit and wait while I input symbols into my computer or point to letters on my alphabet board. People find the silence so hard, they often don't talk to me.

I've been working now for more than six months; I have friends and colleagues; I meet strangers when I go out into the world; and I'm interacting with them all. In doing so, I've learned that people's voices move in a seamless cycle, sentences running one into another while they talk. But I interrupt the rhythm and make it messy. People must make a conscious effort to look at me and listen to what I have to say. They must allow me the space to speak because I can't butt in and many don't want to listen to the silence I create as they wait for me to input words into a computer. I understand why it is hard. We live in a world in which we seldom hear nothing at all. There is usually a television or radio, telephone or car horn to fill the gaps and if not there is meaningless small talk. But a conversation with me is as much about the silences as it is about the words, and I notice if my words are listened to or not because I choose each one so carefully.

I'm not nearly as talkative as I once thought I would be.

When my family chat over dinner, I often stay silent and when colleagues talk about what they did at the weekend, I sometimes don't join in. People don't mean to be unkind; they just don't think to stop and give way to me. They assume I'm taking part in their conversation because I'm in the same room but I'm not. The best time for me to talk is with one person who knows me well enough to pre-empt whatever I'm going to say.

'You want to go to the cinema?' Erica will say as I point to 'C' and 'I'.

'You think she's cute?' she'll ask when I smile at a woman who passes.

'Water?' she'll declare when I bring my drinks grid up on my laptop.

I like it when Erica does this because I'm as keen to take shortcuts as anyone else. Just because my life is lived as slowly as a giant toddler who needs nappies, bottles, straws and a sunhat before he can set foot outside the house doesn't mean I enjoy it that way. That's why I'm glad when people who know me well help me to speed up a little. Others seem to worry that I'll be offended if they butt in while we talk. If only they knew what I would give to enjoy the rapid cut and thrust of the conversations I hear around me.

I often wonder if people think I have any sense of humour at all. Comedy is all in the timing, the rapid delivery and arched eyebrow, and I might just manage the last of that trio but the first two are a serious problem for me. People have to know me well to know that I enjoy joking around and the fact that I'm often so silent means it's easy for them to assume I'm serious. It feels at times as if I'm still someone others create their own character for, just as I was during all the years when

I couldn't communicate. I remain in so many ways a blank page onto which they write their own script.

'You're so sweet,' people will often say.

'What a gentle nature you have!' person after person tells me.

'You are such a kind man,' someone else trills.

If only they knew of the gnawing anxiety, fiery frustration and aching sexual desire that course through my veins at times. I'm not the gentle mute they often think I am; I'm just lucky that I don't unwittingly betray my feelings by snapping in anger or whining in annoyance. So often now I'm aware that I'm a cipher for what other people want to think of me.

The only time I can guarantee they will be keen to know what I'm saying is when I'm not actually talking to them. Children aren't the only ones who reveal their inbuilt voyeurism by staring – adults just hide it better. I'm often stared at as I spell out words on my alphabet board with hands that are still perhaps the most capricious part of my body. While my left hand remains largely unreliable, I can use my right to point at the letters on my alphabet board and operate my computer switches. But I can't hold firmly on to something like a mug. Even though I can lift finger food to my mouth, I can't hold an interloper like a fork for fear I might stab myself because my movement is so jerky. At least I'm getting so fast at using my board now that strangers find it harder and harder to look over my shoulder and listen in.

'He goes too quickly for me!' my mother said with a laugh to a man who'd been staring at us as we chatted in a supermarket queue.

The man looked embarrassed as Mum spoke to him, obviously fearful that he was going to be chastised. But we are so used to being listened to that neither my mother nor I take much notice any more. Despite these difficulties in communicating, I still treasure the fact that I was given the chance to speak at all. I was given an opportunity that I took and without it I wouldn't be where I am now. My rehabilitation is the work of many people – Virna, my parents, the experts at the communication centre – because I would never have been able to talk without their help. Others are not so lucky.

Recently, in the same supermarket where the man tried to listen to my conversation with Mum, we saw an older woman being pushed around in a wheelchair. She looked about fifty. Soon my mother started chatting to her and her carer. Maybe the woman was using sign language or pointing at things but for some reason my mother discovered that she'd lost the power of speech after a stroke.

'Does your family know about all the things that can be done to help you communicate again?' Mum asked the woman before showing her my alphabet board. 'There's so much out there but you have to find it.'

The carer told us the woman had an adult daughter. Mum urged her to explain that she'd met someone who had told her about all the things that could be done for her mother.

'There's no reason why you shouldn't be able to communicate with your daughter again,' Mum said to the woman. 'You just have to find out what works best for you.'

But when we next met, the carer told us that the woman's daughter hadn't done anything about what she'd been told.

'Why don't you give me her phone number?' Mum said. 'I'd be happy to reassure her that she mustn't give up hope or listen to what the doctors say.'

As the carer wrote out the phone number on a piece of paper, I looked at the woman sitting opposite me in her chair.

'G-O-O-D-L-U-C-K,' I spelled out on my alphabet board and she stared at me for the longest moment.

A few days later Mum came back into the living room after calling the woman's daughter.

'I don't think she really wanted to hear from me,' she said. 'She just didn't seem interested.'

We said no more about it. We both knew that the woman would never escape the straitjacket of her own body – she wasn't going to be given the chance to. She'd be silent forever because no one was going to help set her free.

After that, I often thought about the woman and wondered how she was. But whenever I did, I remembered her eyes as she looked at me the last time I saw her in the supermarket. They'd been filled with fear. Now I understood why.

31

The Speech

I can hardly believe I'm here. It's November 2003 and I'm sitting on a low stage in a huge lecture room with my colleague Munyane, who has just addressed the audience in front of us. There must be more than 350 people waiting for me to speak. I've been working at the communication centre for four months now and have been chosen to address a conference of health professionals.

First Munyane gave an overview of AAC and now it's my turn to talk. Even though all I must do is press the button that will make Perfect Paul's voice boom out of the sound system to which my laptop is connected, I don't know if I'll be able to do it. My hands are shaking so much I'm not sure I'll be able to control them.

Somehow I've become an accidental public speaker in recent months and my story has even been featured in the newspapers. It has surprised me that a room full of people at a school or community centre want to hear about me, and I can't think why so many have come today. I wish Erica were here to give me a smile. She's gone back to the States and it's in moments like this that I miss her most. The friendship I treasured so much must now be contained in emails and the door she gave me onto the world has closed.

I should have known this was a big event when Mum and I arrived and were offered lunch from a table covered in more dishes than I'd ever seen before. The prospect of picking exactly what I wanted to eat was almost too much for me and the sticky toffee pudding I'd finished my meal with rolls uneasily in my stomach now as I stare out into the audience.

Munyane smiles.

'They're ready when you are,' she whispers.

I push the tiny lever that controls my new electric wheel-chair and glide to the centre of the stage. Just as Professor Alant predicted, it has made me far more independent. A month before my twenty-eighth birthday, I was finally able to control where I went and when for the first time. Now if I want to leave the room because the television is boring, I can go; if I decide to explore the streets around the house where my parents have lived since I was a child, then I'm able to.

I got the chair after writing an open letter on a website I belong to asking for any suggestions about how to get one because I knew my parents couldn't afford the cost. Over the past few months I've made friends in countries like England and Australia by joining Internet groups and meeting more people in the AAC community. It's a strange but reassuring feeling to know that I have friends in so many places now. Getting to know people via my computer feels liberating. I'm exploring the world and the people I meet don't see my chair: they just know *me*.

But I never expected the Internet to be as powerful as it turned out to be after my letter was seen by someone in Canada who had a relative living not far from me in South Africa. Soon he had contacted me to say that his Round Table group wanted to buy me a new chair with some of the money they'd raised for charity. Words can't express how grateful I am to have it even though I'm not sure everyone around me is quite so pleased.

Controlling my own movement for the first time is interesting, as I totter like a toddler learning to move independently. I've crashed into doors, fallen off pavements and run over the toes of unsuspecting strangers as I've revelled in my new-found liberation.

I've become more independent in other ways too. My colleague Kitty, who is an occupational therapist, has worked with me on tiny details that have made my work life easier. Now I have a new handle on my office door, which means I can open it without help. I've also started wearing weights on my wrists to try to strengthen my muscles and stabilise my hand tremors. I continue to be well acquainted with drinking yoghurt, which means no one has to feed me at lunchtime, and I'm careful never to ask for tea or coffee unless someone offers because I'm determined not to be a drain on anyone. As for my clothes, I'm wearing a shirt and tie today. Soon I'm hoping to get my first suit.

Life is changing in so many ways but perhaps none is more terrifying than this. I look out at the audience again and force myself to breathe deeply. My hands are trembling and I will them to let me control my laptop. Turning my head slowly to the left, I shine the headmouse's infrared beam onto the screen and click on one of my switches.

'I would like you all to stop for a moment and really think about not having a voice or any means to communicate,' my computer voice says. 'You could never say "Pass the salt" or tell someone the really important things like "I love you". You can't tell someone that you're uncomfortable, cold or in pain.

'For a time, when I first discovered what had happened to me, I went through a phase where I would bite myself in frustration at the life I found myself in. Then I just gave up. I became totally and completely passive.'

I hope the pauses I programmed into my speech are enough to help the audience follow what I'm saying. It's hard to listen to synthesised speech when you are used to voices that pause, rise and fall. But there's nothing more that I can do now. The room is quiet as I talk about meeting Virna and my assessment, the hunt for a communication device and the cancellation of the black box. Then I tell them about the months of research into computer software, the money my grandfather GD left to my father when he died that allowed my parents to buy me equipment and the work I've done learning to communicate.

'In 2001 I was at a day centre for the profoundly mentally and physically disabled,' I say. 'Eighteen months ago, I didn't know anything about computers, was completely illiterate and had no friends.

'Now I can operate more than a dozen software programmes, I've taught myself to read and write and I have good friends and colleagues at both of my two jobs.'

I stare out at the rows of faces in front of me. I wonder if

I'll ever be able to convey my experiences to people. Is there a limit to words? A place where they can take us after which there is a no man's land of incomprehension? I can't be sure. But I must at least hope that somehow I can help people to understand if they want to. There are so many eyes on me, hundreds of pairs, and my heart thumps as my computer carries on speaking.

'My life has changed dramatically,' I say. 'But I'm still learning to adjust to it and although people tell me that I'm intelligent, I struggle to believe it. My progress is down to a lot of hard work and the miracle that happened when people believed in me.'

As I timidly look out at the room, I realise that no one is fidgeting or yawning. Everyone is completely still as they listen.

'Communication is one of the things that makes us human,' I say. 'And I am honoured to have been given the chance to do it.'

Finally I fall silent. My speech is over. I've said all that I wanted to say to this room full of strangers. They are silent for a split second. I stare out at them, unsure what to do. But then I hear a noise – the sound of clapping. It's soft at first but the hands beat together louder and louder and I watch as one person and then another gets to their feet. One by one, the crowd rises. I stare at the faces in front of me, people smiling and laughing as they clap, while I sit in the middle of the stage. The sound swells and swells. Soon it's so big that I feel it might suck me under. I stare down at my feet, hardly daring to believe what I'm seeing and hearing. Finally I push the lever of my chair and move to the side of the stage.

'Mr Pistorius?'

The woman who interpreted my speech into sign language for deaf members of the audience is standing in front of me.

'I just wanted to say that you're an inspiration,' she says in a rush. 'You are a truly extraordinary man. To have experienced what you have and remain so positive is an example for us all.'

I can hear how emotional she is as she speaks in a rush and see the strength of her feeling etched on her face.

'Thank you for telling us your story,' she says. 'I feel proud to have been here today.'

Before I can reply another person comes up to congratulate me and then another and another – so many faces stare down at me as they laugh and smile.

'You were wonderful!'

'So inspiring!'

'Your story is just amazing.'

I don't know what to say. I feel shocked and unsure as Munyane smiles at me reassuringly. I can hardly understand why people are reacting this way but as they talk to me I think of a mother I met recently after speaking at a school for disabled children.

'My son is a pupil here and I would be proud if he grew up to be like you,' she told me afterwards.

I didn't understand what she meant at the time but now perhaps I am beginning to. As hands clap my back and congratulations are given, I sit amid the noise and movement and realise that people want to hear the story of the boy who came back from the dead. It amazes them – it amazes me too.

32

A New World

Life and I are in constant collision. At every turn my eyes open in wonder as I crash into another experience: seeing a man with a plume of brightly coloured hair like parrot feathers running down the centre of his head; tasting a cloud of melting sugar called candyfloss that melts on my tongue; feeling the warm pleasure that comes with going shopping for the first time to buy Christmas presents for my family; or the sharp surprise of seeing women dressed in short skirts with faces painted in bright red and blue cosmetics. There is so much to know and I am impatient, eager, starving for all the information I can gather.

In January 2004, a few months after I gave my speech, I started working four days a week – two at the communication centre and two at the health centre. I do everything from editing newsletters and maintaining computer networks to meeting other AAC users. I'm even learning how to build websites and have been accepted onto a university course after Professor Alant encouraged me to apply for it.

I have no memory of school and my textbooks will have to be dictated onto tapes because I can't yet read well enough to study them. The rest of my fellow students, however, will be postgraduates – many of them teachers. I won't get a full degree because I haven't graduated from high school but I'll be awarded an advanced certificate in education if I finish the course. The course is about the theory and practice of educating those with AAC needs and I'll need to study every spare minute that I'm not at work in order to keep up.

I'm finally daring to dream that independence might be within my reach. Work and study are what will help me get a better job, a higher income and maybe even a home of my own one day. These are the things I want and I must do my best to achieve them.

'Look at you,' Diane Bryen said with a smile when we saw each other at a conference. It was a gathering of AAC users from all over Africa and experts from around the world. I was one of the speakers, as was Diane.

'You were so fearful when I first met you,' she said. 'But now you're beginning to roar!'

Change is hard to see when it's your own. I'd never stopped to notice the person I was becoming until I attended Diane's workshop for the second time and she asked us to draw a picture of our dreams. Virna was assisting me at the conference. As the pencil in her hand hovered over a blank sheet of paper, I told her what I dreamed of. In strong, bright strokes, she captured my hopes on the paper: I watched as she drew a house with a picket fence around it and a dog wagging its tail. This is what I wanted and when I thought about having a life so much my own, it made me feel as if I was soaring inside.

A few days after I returned to work, I was sitting with Virna during our lunch break at the health centre when she turned towards me.

'I hardly know who you are any more,' she said.

I looked at her, unsure what she meant, and nothing more was said. But I continued to feel confused as I thought about it in the days that followed because I'd always thought Virna was the person who knew me best in the world. Although my feelings for her remain as strong as ever, I've been careful not to reveal them again. Instead I've talked to Virna as a friend about my deepest secrets and fears, and described to her all the emotions I have as I go out into the world. That's why I couldn't understand when she said she didn't recognise me.

Now I wonder if learning to communicate more will change the things I thought would always stay the same. Virna has always rejoiced in the new person I'm becoming. But does she find it hard to recognise a man who is finally beginning to see a world without her as its axis? She kept me grounded for so long. Now I'm beginning to fly – but I'm spreading my wings alone.

33

The Laptop

I stare at my laptop. The screen has gone blank. Terror fills me. I can feel it creep and crawl, scrabble and scratch over my heart. I've been having problems with my laptop for a while and out of politeness sent an email to everyone I knew earlier this evening warning them that something like this might happen. But I never thought my link to the world would actually be lost and I'd suddenly go silent.

I know enough about computers to suspect this is terminal. My laptop is completely lifeless, flatlined. I feel sick. If I don't have my computer, then I can't send text messages or emails, do college assignments or finish off the work I bring home from the office in the evenings to make sure I keep on top of everything. I can't laugh and joke with my friends online, tell them about my day and ask about theirs. I can't describe to them how I'm feeling or make plans to meet up. My physical world might still be limited to the home and office but there are parts of my life that know no boundaries as I chat to people on different continents. All I'll have to communicate with now is a battered old alphabet board that won't reach around the globe the way I need it to.

Panic turns my stomach in cartwheels. My life is ruled by the press of a single button. It stands and falls on a network of wires and I will never know when they're about to go wrong. They aren't like a body that can give me a sign, such as a spike in temperature, a rush of sickness or a sudden pain. Instead, I must spend the rest of my life relying on a hunk of metal that might give up suddenly without a hint of warning.

I can hardly breathe. My life is so fragile. I've spent all this time thinking that I'd left the ghost boy behind forever. It's only now that I realise how closely he still shadows me.

34

The Counsellor

'How are you feeling today, Martin?'

I look at the counsellor sitting opposite me. I'm not really sure what he's expecting me to say. I stare at my laptop and click on three symbols.

'I am well, thank you,' my voice intones.

'Good,' the counsellor says with a smile. 'Can you remember what we were talking about the last time you came to see me?'

I'm not sure. Do we ever actually talk during the hour I spend in this office each week? We speak, of course — the counsellor sitting behind his glass desk in a sturdy, black office chair that sways to and fro when he leans back, me on the other side in my wheelchair with a laptop in front of me. But I'm not sure if this exchange of words is really talking.

When I'm here, I often think of a film I once saw on TV called *Short Circuit*. It's about a robot that developed a human personality and an insatiable desire to understand the world around him. No one, except for the girl who rescued him after he ran away from the laboratory where he'd been created, believed he could really have feelings. He was just a machine, after all. He couldn't be something he wasn't.

As time passes, I feel more and more like that robot because the counsellor, like other people, doesn't seem to know quite what to make of me when I try to communicate. I didn't notice it when I first rejoined the world because in the rush of excitement at being able to say even a few words, I didn't see clearly how other people responded to me. But now I watch the counsellor staring at the ceiling and checking his nails as he waits for me to talk, or hear him rush on with the conversation as I'm left trailing in his wake, trying to answer a question he asked ten sentences ago, and I'm filled with frustration – just as I often am when I speak to people now.

I feel more and more bewildered by a world that I often don't understand. When I was a ghost boy, I could understand people: if they dismissed, doubted or undermined each other, I could see it; if they praised, teased or were shy, I could tell. But I'm no longer an outsider. I see things from a different perspective now. It's impossible at times to recognise how people are behaving towards me as I try to interact with them. All my reference points have changed. It's as if I can only calibrate others when they have nothing to do with me: if someone is rude, I don't realise it; if they are impatient, I can't see it.

When Mum and I went out shopping recently, we met a woman whose son had been in my class at school.

'How's Martin?' she asked my mother.

The woman didn't even glance at me.

'Why don't you ask him?' Mum replied.

But the woman couldn't bring herself to make eye contact or ask me a simple question. It seemed almost normal to me because after so many years of being invisible, it's sometimes hard even now to remember that I'm not. My mother was livid at the way the woman had treated me, and it was only her reaction that helped me to understand someone had slighted me.

It happens a lot. When a TV crew came to film at the communication centre, I knew something bad had happened after Professor Alant introduced me to the producer.

'I'm from Canada,' he said in a very loud voice, carefully enunciating each syllable. 'It's a very long way away.'

I stared at the man, unsure why he was telling me something so obvious in such a loud voice. Only my colleagues' outraged expressions told me that he had been rude.

My mother is the one who decided that I should see the counsellor after I told my parents a little about what had happened to me during all my years in institutions. She believes I'm angry about what I told her, which is why I should talk to someone. But all I want is to move forward instead of look back. Nevertheless I'm brought here each week to see the counsellor. After my mother has accompanied me into his office and checked my laptop is working properly, she leaves us alone as I try to make sense of all that has happened.

'You have to accept that you are very intelligent,' the counsellor tells me again and again.

I never know what to say when he says this. It's as if the words won't permeate my brain. The concept is too big for me to fit into my consciousness. I spent years being treated as an imbecile and now the man paid to be my friend tells me I'm clever?

'Most people have ways to express their emotions,' he says. 'They can slam doors or shout and swear. But you only have words, Martin, and that makes it hard to show your feelings.'

Then he sits back in his chair, looks at me seriously and I'm at a loss once again about what I'm supposed to say. It feels like I'm trying to play a game but I'm missing all the clues. Although I send the counsellor an email each day telling him how I feel, just as he asked me to, he rarely replies. Then, when I see him, he talks in platitudes I don't understand. It makes me wonder if he's really interested in what I think or if I'm just a case study to be intrigued by. Will he help me solve the problems that I never even considered I'd have when I dreamed of being able to speak? Or will I end up as the subject of a scholarly study about the man without a voice?

The counsellor stares at the ceiling as he waits for me to speak. What can I say? That I thought my life would change completely when I started to communicate and now I know it isn't going to? That my greatest challenge is not learning to communicate but being listened to? That people don't hear what they don't want to and I have no way of making them listen?

I look at him, frozen by indecision. I know I must try to discuss emotions that I buried deep within myself years ago, dig up a past I'm still trying to outrun each night when I fall asleep. Although I've talked a little about the past to my parents, I understand it is a minefield they don't want to cross with me for fear of triggering an explosion. I, too, am scared of destroying the fragile peace we've created together. I don't want words, even those spoken to a stranger in an anonymous room, to open up a Pandora's box I'll never be able to close again. But I know I must try to communicate some of what I've seen; I must attempt to put it into words for this man who sits so still and silent in front of me.

My pulse races at the thought of confession. What happened to me is a darkness that is always with me and I fear I will be tormented forever if I don't try to speak of it.

35

Memories

'Eat it, you fucking donkey,' the carer snaps.

I stare at the mince lying grey on the spoon in front of me. I am twenty-one years old and still the ghost boy.

'Eat it!'

I open my mouth and burning hot food is shovelled in. A rancid taste fills my mouth. Bile rises in my throat. I force myself to swallow.

'And another.'

I open my mouth obediently. I must think of something else if I'm to persuade my stomach to accept what it is being fed. I look around the room. The jarringly soft strains of classical violins play in the background as I look at the other children here. Some cry; others are silent. My throat burns as I swallow.

'Hurry up, you heap of rubbish. We'll be here for hours if you don't speed up.'

The metal spoon crashes against my teeth as she forces another mouthful into me. I wish she would leave me hungry, but I know she won't.

'Eat up!'

She pulls my hair – two short tugs that make my eyes water – before she raises another spoon of food towards my mouth. My lips close around it and my heart starts to race as I swallow. I can feel nausea rising inside me. I can't be sick. I breathe deeply.

'Come on, freak. What's wrong with you tonight?'

She lifts up another spoonful of food and a thick smell washes over me. Too late to choke it back down, I can feel the vomit surging up and there is nothing I can do to stop it, however desperately I want to.

'You piece of shit!' the woman screams as I'm sick all over myself and the plate in front of me.

She slaps me around the face. She is so close that I can feel her breath hot on my cheek.

'Do you think you're clever?' the woman screams. 'Do you think you can get out of eating just by puking up?'

I watch as she pushes the spoon towards my plate. She guides it through the vomit and fills the spoon to the brim before raising it to my mouth.

'Eat!'

I open my mouth. I have no other choice. I must force myself to swallow the food that my body has just rejected, praying that it won't do so again or worse will happen. The woman has done this before; she will do it again. I've learned that I can't cry because it only makes her angrier. As the spoon is rammed into my mouth, I hear peals of laughter. I fight down the nausea that is rising once again inside me. The woman smiles, relishing her triumph.

That is the reason why I hated the home in the country so much: one woman there tormented me while other carers laughed. Some days I was just pinched or slapped; on others I was abandoned outside in the blazing heat or left to freeze after being taken out of the bath, shivering until she finally decided to dress me.

There were times when I wondered if she scared herself with her own violence: after giving me an enema so forcefully I bled, she put me into the bath and I watched the water turn bright red. After getting me out, she dipped a toothbrush into the filthy water before cleaning my teeth with it. Later, after she'd set me on the toilet, I stared at the water turning red once more below me and thanked God that I was going to die, smiling at the irony that a bleeding arsehole would be the thing to finish me off.

If I flinched when she touched me, she'd hit me so hard the wind would be knocked out of my lungs. Or she'd smack me on the back of the head if I cried after being left sitting in my own dirt for so long that my skin turned a livid red.

Each day I'd count down the minutes until it was over and I was another twenty-four hours closer to going home. Usually I was at the care centre for only a few days but some-times my stay was as long as six weeks, and panic filled me whenever I heard the phone ring. Was it a call to say my par-ents had been killed in a car accident? Would I be left here forever, a prisoner in an institution where no one would remember me? The fear would build inside me day by day until I could almost taste it. When my mother or father finally came to pick me up, I listened helplessly as they were told I'd had another good stay.

Even when I went home I found it hard not to be afraid because I would soon start to wonder when I'd have to go back again. I wasn't taken there often – maybe once or twice a year – but each time I was put into the car and driven out of the city, I'd start to cry as I realised where we were going. When we crossed over a railway line, I knew we were nearing the home and I'd listen to rocks ricocheting off the bottom of the car as we drove along a dirt road littered with them. As my heart beat and my throat tightened, I would long to scream, and wondered if I could make my parents hear my thoughts if only I tried hard enough.

But the one thing I wished for more than anything as I sat strapped in a seat, powerless to tell anyone about what I knew would soon happen to me, was for someone to look at me. Surely then they would see what was written on my face? Fear. I knew where I was. I knew where I was going. I had feelings. I wasn't just a ghost boy. But no one looked.

36

Lurking in Plain Sight

Similar things happened in other places too, where children and adults were too weak, silent or mentally defenceless to tell their secrets. I learned that the people who play out their darkest desires on us, however fleetingly, aren't always the most easily recognisable. They aren't bogey men or women; they are ordinary, forgettable people. Maybe they are even entirely blameless until the chance to use a seemingly empty vessel encourages them to cross a line they might otherwise never have dared breach.

Sometimes it was nothing more than a feeling, as if an invisible line had been overstepped, which made me feel unsafe. I couldn't explain it properly because even though I was a young man, there was so much I didn't understand.

'Kiss, kiss,' one woman whispered in a breathy voice that no one else could hear as she bent her head towards me. She sounded flirtatious, like a girl tempting an embrace from an unwilling suitor.

On another occasion, the mother of a child I knew came into a room as I was lying alone and naked from the waist down, waiting to be changed.

What's this?' she said as she scratched my penis gently.

The incident was over as soon as it began because a carer came back to the room. But it made me feel confused, unsure, and I didn't know what to make of the troubled feelings that filled me.

It wasn't always like this though. Sometimes it was only too clear what was happening and fear would wash over me as I realised I was being attacked in a way that I could never defend myself against.

'Look at you,' a carer once said as she bathed me.

The next day I watched silently as she looked around the empty room, lifted up her dress and straddled my hip before rubbing herself against me. I lay unmoving, unblinking, unseeing, until I felt her weight rise off me. I was left with the gnawing fear that she might touch me again but she didn't.

What was I to these women – a perverse fantasy long held and buried or a moment of madness? I can't be sure. But to another woman who also abused me for several years, I know I was never more than a thing, an object to be used as and when she wished before being dropped again.

Solitude was the oxygen that gave life to her behaviour: she always found a way for us to be alone. The first time she touched me, I knew with absolute clarity what she was doing as I felt her hand push questioningly at the crotch of my trousers. It was as if she was afraid, uncertain, and the incident was brief. But she was bolder the next time, as her hands lingered on my penis. Soon she had become even braver, as if realising that opening the door to this darkness wasn't as terrifying as she'd thought it might be.

Sometimes she would wrap her legs around my body and thrust against me harder and harder until I heard her gasp. Or she would stand behind me as I lay on my back and pull my arms above my head so that my hands rested against her thighs. As my fingers trembled uncontrollably, just as she knew they would, I would hear her breathing become ragged as she pushed my fingers against her sex.

She was usually silent when she took her fill of me. Sometimes it would go on for what felt like forever as she rocked and pressed herself against me, her body jerking mine in time with hers, until she was finally still. Each time, I would try to lose myself in the quiet, closing myself down inside. Yet still I could feel my soul freezing over. It was only later that feelings of shame filled me.

If she spoke to me at all, it was as a child would speak to a doll she knows isn't really there.

'Let's fidget,' she whispered once as she pulled me out of my wheelchair.

The one thing she always made sure of was that I could never see her.

'You shouldn't be looking,' she said as she turned my head to face away from her. But it wasn't me she spoke to: it was herself.

It didn't happen all the time. Sometimes weeks or months went by before she touched me again and then it would happen on several consecutive meetings. It was worse that way because I never knew what she was going to do or when.

Nothing made me feel more powerless as I waited for her to come for me again. Anxiety about what she might do when I saw her next would build up inside me as I wondered whether I would escape this time or not. Fear threw a veil across my days. I knew I couldn't stop her or speak out. I was just an unresponsive object that she used as and when she wanted, the blank canvas onto which she painted her black appetites. And so I would sit and wait, listening until I heard her voice again, knowing that the moment I did, I'd never more desperately want to run.

'Hello, Martin,' she says with a smile as she looks down at me.

I stare at her. My stomach turns with nausea. I can feel a scream unfurling inside me like a flag snapping in the wind but I can't let it out.

'Off we go,' she says and I feel my chair begin to move.

She takes me into a room where no one will see us and lies me down on a bench. Lifting one foot off the floor and resting it beside me, she keeps her other foot on the ground as she lifts her skirt. She lowers herself down, pressing herself against the big toe of my left foot as she starts to move rhythmically against me. I try to disappear.

Later I lie unmoving as she sits down beside me. She reads a magazine, flicking through the pages absent-mindedly while picking her nose. Eventually she looks at her watch and stands up. But just as she prepares to leave, she turns again. She has remembered something.

I watch as she drags her finger slowly down the arm of my T-shirt, wiping herself off on me. A trail of mucus glistens on my sleeve. Her contempt is complete now.

Sometimes she lies beside me, at others on top of me. Sometimes she touches herself, at others she touches me. But whatever happens, I'm nothing to her, forgotten until she decides to come for me, while she never leaves me. She is an ogre residing in my dreams, chasing me and screeching, tormenting and terrifying me. Night after night, I wake up sweating and terrified after she's come to me again as I've slept. She is a parasite that has wormed its way into my soul. As I lie in the dark, I wonder if I will ever be rid of her.

37

Fantasies

It was at this time more than any other that I needed to rely on my imagination. If my fantasy world had one recurring theme it was escape, because I could be anything I dared to be and more: not just a pirate but a pilot, a space raider or a Formula One driver, a merman, a secret agent or a Jedi warrior with mind-reading powers.

Sometimes I'd sit in my wheelchair in my classroom at the care centre and feel myself shrinking as I left the world behind. As the chair got bigger and bigger, I'd imagine myself to be as small as a toy soldier, so tiny I could fit into the jet plane waiting for me in the corner of the room. To everyone else it might look like a toy but I alone knew it was a fighter jet and the engines were running, ready for me.

In my dreams, my body was always strong. I'd leap up out of my wheelchair before looking around as I listened for footsteps. If someone saw me, they'd be shocked. I was ready to fight back. They might think that I was a trick of their imagination but I wasn't; I was real. Throwing myself off the edge of the chair and landing on the floor with a soft thump, I looked down to see that my T-shirt and shorts had disappeared and I was wearing a grey flying suit. It rustled as I ran over to the jet, climbed up the steps and wriggled in behind the controls as I put on my helmet. Engines growled and lights flashed in front of me but I didn't worry. I understood why they did this because I was a trained fighter pilot.

I pushed a lever forward and the plane started to move. Faster and faster, it raced across the lino floor of my class-room before lifting into the air and flying into the corridor. Marietta was walking towards me but I sped around her head. I was too fast and small for her to see as I pulled the lever again and the plane shot forward.

I was thrown back by the G-force as a trolley reared up ahead of me and, as I darted to miss it, I knew that one wrong move would clip my jet's wings and send me crashing to the ground. But my hand stayed steady. Bam! I flew out the other side of the trolley towards the doors leading outside.

They were closing as I approached them so I flipped the plane on its side. The jet rushed cleanly between the doors as they creaked closed and I was free. The sky above me was blue and the outside world smelled of dust and sun. I nosed the plane upwards, knowing that soon I would be high enough to look down at the earth below me: splots of green and splashes of brown rushing past. I pulled the lever back as far as it could go – full throttle, sonic thrusters on max – and the jet shot up into the sky in a corkscrew. It spun me round and round.

My head was dizzy but I felt light. I started laughing.

Roger and out – I was free.

Below, the highway was filled with cars and people going home from work. I knew where the roads would take me if I followed them – home.

When I lay in bed at the care home in the country I'd think of the train tracks nearby and imagine myself stealing outside, running through the long brown grass of the Highveld. In the distance, I'd see a train pulling faded brown goods carriages behind it, some covered in tarpaulins, some open and filled with glistening black coal. Running towards the train, I'd grab on to the last carriage just before it disappeared down the line. I didn't know where the train would take me. All I cared about was that I was leaving.

Water was another thing I loved to dream about, fantasising that it would rush into whatever room I was sitting in, lift me up and bear me away on the crest of a wave. In the water, I would duck and dive, my body free and strong. Or I'd imagine that my wheelchair had grown James Bond wings and I'd soar into the sky as the care staff stared up, open-mouthed, unable to prevent me from flying away.

In my fantasy world, I was still the child I'd been when I first fell asleep. The only thing that changed as I grew older was that I started to imagine myself as a world-famous cricket player because I'd cultivated an interest in the sport as I watched Dad and David enjoy it.

My brother was very good at cricket and would tell Mum, Dad and Kim about his latest match when he came home. I so wanted to share something with him. David always made me smile by telling me jokes, talking in funny voices or tickling me, so I started listening intently whenever the cricket came on the radio or TV.

Soon I could lose days and weeks in matches that I imagined going on in my head. Each one would start with me sitting in a silent changing room as I laced up my shoes before stepping outside into the sunshine. As I walked across the pitch, I'd rub the ball on the edge of my shirt before checking to see if it was shiny enough and I'd stare at the batsman as the crowd hushed. I didn't feel scared by all the people watching me. All I could think of was running down the wicket and feeling the ball, round and solid in my hand, before I flung it at the batsman.

A flash of cherry red would fly through the air as the ball shot out of my hand and I heard the soft click of bails flying off the stumps as the crowd roared. I wasn't always a sure shot, though. Sometimes I'd miss the batsman completely with a ball that went wildly off course, or I'd be bowled out for a duck, which meant I'd walk off the pitch knowing I hadn't done so well that day. But somehow it didn't matter because I was a sporting star. I lived in matches like these day after day as the South African team's most famous all-rounder, who saved the game more often than he lost it. The games became almost endless, over after over of balls were bowled and wickets were won or lost as I retreated from reality.

The one person I talked to was God but He wasn't part of my fantasy world. He was real to me, a presence inside and around that calmed and reassured me. Just as North American Indians might commune with their spirit guides or pagans look to the seasons and the sun, I spoke to God as I tried to make sense of what had happened to me and asked Him to protect me from harm. God and I didn't talk about the big things in life — we didn't engage in philosophical debates or argue about religion — but I talked to Him endlessly because I knew we shared something important. I didn't have proof that He existed but I believed in Him anyway because I knew He was real. God did the same for me. Unlike people, He didn't need proof that I existed — He knew I did.

38

A New Friend

The noise is like a train gathering speed in the distance. It gets louder and louder until suddenly it explodes into the room – a ball of yellow fur, a huge red tongue and sodden paws that leaps onto the sofa, drenching it in seconds. A huge tail wags frenziedly and big brown eyes stare around the room.

'Kojak! Down!'

The dog takes no notice as he carries on looking around before finally taking a flying leap off the sofa towards me. I could swear he's smiling.

'Kojak! No!'

The dog doesn't listen to a word his owner is saying to him. All he wants is to say hello to the strange man sitting in the strange chair.

'Get down!'

The man drags the huge yellow Labrador off me and wrestles him to a sitting position. But even pinned to his master's side with a firm hand on his collar, the dog keeps moving. He waves his head around wildly and wriggles his bottom. His tongue lolls out of his mouth because even his breath can't keep up with him.

I look at Mum and Dad. I've never seen them look scared before.

'So this is the dog that you're looking to rehome?' my father says in a neutral voice.

'Yes,' the man replies. 'We're moving to Scotland and want to find him a new family. He's such a loving dog. I'm sorry he's so wet. Kojak just loves the swimming pool!'

Horror steals its way onto my mother's face like a blind being drawn down a window. I know that she dares not let herself speak.

'He's had all his injections and we've done some obedience training with him,' the man continues. 'Obviously, he's only eight months old so he's still full of energy.'

As if on cue, Kojak wrenches against his master's grip as a volley of barks explode from him. I almost expect my mother to start screaming.

'What do you think, Martin?' Dad asks me.

I stare at the dog. He is too big and boisterous, obviously deaf to any kind of command and will wreak havoc in my parents' neat home. In four months of searching, I've never seen a dog like him but, even so, something tells me that he's the one for me.

I smile at Dad.

'Well, I think Martin has made his mind up,' he says.

'That's great news!' Kojak's owner exclaims. 'You won't regret it.'

I look at Mum. I think she's trying not to cry.

39

Will He Ever Learn?

I've never forgotten Pookie, which is why I want a dog so much. I've always remembered the bond we shared and I want a companion just like her. I want something to care for that isn't aware of all my limits and defects. Despite my enthusiasm, my mother doesn't like the idea. She doesn't want something else to look after, let alone a huge dog that will trail hair and mud in its wake.

Kim was the one who in the end came to my rescue when she was home on a visit from the UK earlier this year. She quickly saw that I was working harder than ever – literally day and night at times – and sometimes getting just four or five hours' sleep as I tried to keep up with everything.

It's now April 2005 – almost four years since I was first assessed – and in that time I've never stopped working. It's as if I can't allow myself to let go of life for a second after being given a chance at it. I don't have a social life or hobbies. All I do is work as I struggle not just to keep up but to carry on improving. Because I was static for so long, I want to keep moving forward. I still can't believe that people are giving me opportunities. I constantly feel afraid that I might be found out as inexperienced at life so I work hard to make up for what I believe I lack because I feel like a fraud.

After being put in charge of redesigning the communication centre's website, I was seconded from my job there to a scientific research institute where I helped create disability-related Internet resources. It opened up a new world of possibilities for me and I left my job at the health centre. I'm now working three days a week at the communication centre and two as a computer technologist at the scientific research institute.

Outside office hours, I continue to raise awareness about AAC and I've joined the executive committee of a national organisation for people like me with little or no functioning speech. I even took my first-ever flight in January to do a whistle-stop tour of five cities nationwide for a charity fundraising event. It made me wonder why birds ever come down to earth because my body felt so free when the plane took off.

If I'm not doing paid or voluntary work, I'm studying.

But all this activity is why Kim knew something had to change when she came to visit. She could see there was little else in my life other than work so she talked to Mum and Dad, who agreed I could get a dog.

'You'll have to take care of it, though,' Mum warned. 'Feed it and clean it. I'm already looking after four people in this house so the dog will be your responsibility.'

'I won't ask you to do a thing,' I told her, although I had

yet to understand just what taking an enthusiastic young Labrador for a walk in a wheelchair would really mean.

That was how the search for Kojak started. Although people wanted me to get something small, my heart was set on a yellow Labrador because they seemed to me to be the happiest dogs of all. I looked at some litters but saw many puppies that were too sickly while others had some physical characteristic that told me they hadn't been bred correctly. I couldn't afford a top of the range pedigree dog so I waited several months to find the one that would be the perfect fit for me. I then got a tip from a breeder about one she'd sold that now needed a new home. The moment I saw Kojak, I knew he was meant to be mine.

Taking care of a wild child like him is proving to be more difficult than I expected. From the moment he arrived, Kojak has caused controversy. Seconds after I shut the front door, he bounded off to sniff every nook and cranny of his new home and sent a cup of tea flying with his tail as he ran into the living room. As my parents got up from their armchairs to clear up the mess, Kojak leaped onto Dad's chair.

'Get down!' shrieked my mother.

Kojak did as he was told – then jumped onto Mum's chair. With just one look, he'd understood the pecking order in our house.

'Will we ever get control of this dog?' Mum asked wearily. I, too, wondered if we would later that evening, after Kojak had been locked in the kitchen while we ate supper.

'What has he done?' Mum roared when she walked into the kitchen and found the floor covered in cooking oil and vomit.

Kojak had gulped down most of a bottle of oil so

enthusiastically that it had reappeared almost immediately. Even so he still looked as if he was smiling. As my mother raged, the two of us went outside. We didn't go back in until I knew she'd gone to bed and the coast was clear.

That's the kind of dog Kojak is: intelligent but charmingly troublesome; clever enough to understand when he's being naughty and desperate to please but somehow unable to do so always. His chewing budget has threatened to rage out of control, as he has gobbled up mobile phones, disappeared with several TV remote controls and destroyed almost every established plant in my parents' garden.

'It's been Kojaked,' my mother says now with a sigh when she looks at the craters in her flower border, because for some reason he can't get enough of a clump of bright orange birds of paradise flowers that she was once proud of.

Kojak's idiosyncrasies don't stop there. If a car window is opened, he'll try to climb out of it, and he can't sit still long enough to have a pee, which means that he hops from foot to foot as he does it, like a boxer preparing for a fight. He's also knocked over my wheelchair several times after lunging at something and pulling me over. Whether it's a dog barking or a new smell, he can't resist investigating, and he wants to jump in and save me whenever I get into our swimming pool. He made a break for freedom one day during an obedience training class only to find a five-foot drop on the other side of the wall that he'd jumped over. Suspended in mid-air by his lead, Kojak stared at me as if pleading for his life with an executioner while Dad rescued him with the help of the woman who ran the training class. The other dogs just looked on in despair.

I know, however, that buried deep within Kojak is a sensible dog trying its hardest to come out. I knew even before I got him that the only hope I had of having any kind of control over a dog was by teaching him some rules so I'd signed us up for obedience training classes. Kojak is now learning to respond to non-verbal commands and each weekend my mother or father takes the two of us to dog school, where we are slowly learning to understand each other.

Raising my fist to my chest tells Kojak to sit down, while a finger pointed at the ground instructs him to lie flat. A fist held next to my body asks him to get up again and a hand held straight up tells him to wait. Happily, he has quickly learned the basics and we've moved on to the more playful stuff: if I wave at him now, he waves his paw back; if I hold up my hand, he bats it with his paw in a 'high five'; and if I hold out my hand, he raises his paw so he can shake it.

It's taking time but I'm sure Kojak is slowly calming down. He's even learned some service skills, such as opening doors and closing drawers for me. These can sometimes be haphazard because teaching him to take off my socks has given him such a taste for them that he now steals every pair he can find in the washing basket. Teaching him to do things around the house also sparked the idea of teaching him to ring the doorbell and he has taken to running off just so he can come home and let us know he's back.

But whatever his shortcomings, Kojak is what I wanted him to be: a companion who always makes me smile with his unfailing cheerfulness and loving nature. Whatever mistakes he makes, his presence has made my world a far happier place.

40

GD and Mimi

My grandparents, GD and Mimi, taught me perhaps my most important lesson about love: if it's true, it will last a lifetime and if it's strong enough, it can be passed from generation to generation.

I'd heard stories about GD and Mimi all my life: how GD won a medal for bravery at the age of sixteen after diving off rocks into the sea to save a drowning woman and how Mimi loved dances so much when she was a girl that she would travel miles to attend them. GD, who was working as a trainee miner when they met, would cycle thirty miles to see Mimi. He was so determined to provide her with a good life after she'd agreed to marry him that he took his mining exams eleven times in order to qualify as a manager. GD was the youngest of sixteen children and Mimi was the eldest of four so it was perhaps inevitable that they would want kids of their own and soon they had my father and his two sisters. While Mimi taught her children to do the Charleston as she ran their home, GD built a house for his family so they could move out of mining accommodation.

My grandparents lived together happily for almost sixty years and continued to do so even after Mimi was confined to bed when she fell and broke her hip soon after my awareness started to return. She never got up again but Mimi ran her home like a sergeant-major from the comfort of her bed. GD was told what to buy at the shops, how to cook it and when to take his heart medication. He could never see the irony when he went to visit 'the old dears' in the local home for pensioners.

I loved them both very much. Whenever we went to visit, my wheelchair would be put next to Mimi's bed so she could reach out to take my hands in hers. Staring at her paper-thin skin, which looked so delicate I thought it might tear, I wondered if I would ever grow so ancient. But then, when I was twenty-three, Mimi fell ill and this time there was nothing that could be done. Her body was simply wearing out. As she got weaker and weaker, I'd watch Mimi slip in and out of consciousness as I sat beside her.

My grandfather seemed lost. It was during one of those final visits that I heard him tell my father what he wanted more than anything in the world.

'I'd like to sleep next to my wife one last time,' GD said, because Mimi had been so ill that he hadn't been able to.

Two days later, the phone rang at home and Dad picked it up. He talked quietly for a few moments before putting it down.

'Mimi has died,' he said and I watched him walk up the passageway with his hands held behind his head, as if trying to massage the realisation that he'd lost his mother into his skull.

I was filled with sadness for my father as he put me into the car and drove us to his parents' home to see Mimi for the last time. She was lying on the bed when we got there and my father kissed her as I watched. No one knew that I completely understood what had happened, of course, and I longed to comfort GD as he cried while we all sat waiting for the undertakers to arrive.

'I feel as if my arm has been amputated,' he sobbed and I knew his heart was breaking for the woman he'd loved for so many years and now lost.

Their love had lasted a lifetime; their stories had become woven together so tightly that they'd forgotten where one ended and another began. All around us were scattered the tiny clues of their love, enmeshed in even the most mundane objects like the winter coat my father and aunts found in Mimi's wardrobe. GD had spent precious money on his wife because he was anxious to keep her warm.

A few days later Dad spoke at Mimi's funeral about the love she had passed on to her children. When he was a boy, he told the congregation, his mother had knitted his clothes in 'love stitches' and her calm, quiet presence was always with him. One day when he was a small boy helping her to bottle peaches, my father had accidentally spilled burning syrup on Mimi, which had instantly blistered her skin, but she didn't get cross or shout. Instead, she simply washed the burn in cold water, bandaged it and quietly carried on.

As I listened to my father, I realised that I was learning another lesson about the love I'd seen between men and women: sometimes it was playful like Henk and Arrietta's, sometimes peaceful like Ingrid and Dave's, but if you were lucky, it could last forever just as it had between GD and Mimi. That kind of love can be passed from one person to the next, like a life force that will comfort anyone it touches and create memories that burn strong years after the events that inspired them.

This was the kind of love my father had known and now, as he spoke, I knew he could see his mother in his mind's eye as clearly as he had when she was still alive. As he remembered that moment in his childhood, he could feel her touch and hear her voice as once more he became a boy enveloped in love on the day he bottled peaches with his mother.

41

Loving Life and Living Love

The waves roll onto the beach as the smell of fried chicken wafts on the salty wind. My mouth waters as I lift another piece of meat to my mouth. How good it tastes.

It's December 2006 and I'm sitting on the edge of a beach in Cape Town with my friend Graham. He became a fellow AAC user after suffering a bilateral brain stem stroke while he was working on an island off the coast of South Africa more than two decades ago. After Graham was airlifted to hospital, he woke up only to be told that he was paralysed from the eyes down. He was twenty-five.

Today Graham can't move or talk yet he lives life roaring like a lion at anyone who doubts him. Completely physically dependent on others, he refused to go home to be cared for by his mother as he was expected to do after he was paralysed. She lived on the other side of the country, after all, and Graham wanted to continue to live in Cape Town. So he went into a nursing home, where he still lives today, and I've never met anyone whose love of life is so infectious.

He lives every minute and loves to break rules: I'm pretty sure that he'll soon ask to be given a mouthful of fried chicken even though he isn't supposed to eat solid food. I understand the kind of longing that's too strong to deny. 'You can't do everything the doctors tell you to,' he says to anyone who might question him. He's told me that it's not just the taste but the physical act of chewing and swallowing he craves. That's why the advice of doctors gets forgotten every now and again as Graham treasures eating a small mouthful of food.

We first met at a conference about eighteen months ago, and I'm in Cape Town now because we're giving speeches at an event tomorrow. But first we have come to the beach to sit side by side like metal birds on a wire and watch the sea. As I chew my chicken, I think of a photograph Graham showed me earlier.

'She's an acquaintance,' he said as I looked at the beautiful woman smiling into the camera lens.

Graham's eyes twinkled as he used the infrared pointer that tracks the tiny movements he can make with his head to operate his communication device and talk to me. I wished I had a picture to show him too, a photo of a woman I love. But I don't and I'm beginning to fear that I never will because, lesson by painful lesson, I'm learning that few women can see past the body that encases me.

I don't know if my longing for love was always a part of me or whether its seeds were sown on a day I can still remember vividly although it was over ten years ago. It was late afternoon when a group of nursing students visited the care home and I was lying on a mattress when I felt someone kneel down beside me. As a straw was put into my mouth, I looked up to see a young woman. Long brown hair framed her face and suddenly I was filled with a longing so strong it almost made me gasp when I felt the gentleness in her hands. I wished I could stretch that tiny moment into forever as the girl who smelled of flowers and sunshine became the world to me. Was it that or all I saw between Henk and Arrietta, Dave and Ingrid, GD and Mimi that coaxed the longing for love to life inside me? Or perhaps it was because of the years of devotion my parents showed me, my brother, my sister and each other.

Whatever the reason, my yearning for love burned stronger still when I started to communicate and it's only now that I can see how naive I've been. I really did believe that I could will love into existence if I wanted it enough and I would find someone to share the kind of feelings I'd seen as a ghost boy. Then Virna taught me that it was going to be far harder than I'd thought at first and I tried to accept the lesson. But although I've run from my feelings and buried them in work, and counted my blessings one by one, there are times now when I feel as lonely as I did before I could communicate.

I realised long ago that my love for Virna was a myth I wrote for myself, a sprite of my own creation that I'd never have been able to capture for real. Whatever I thought, she only ever saw me as a friend and I can't blame her for that. But I didn't learn the lessons she inadvertently tried to teach and I've repeated the same mistake again and again. Although I'm thirty now, there are times when I think I have as much understanding of women as I did when I was a twelve-year-old boy submerged in darkness.

Earlier this year, I travelled with my father to a conference in Israel and sat in a darkened auditorium listening to a professor talk about the challenges facing people like me in having romantic relationships. However much I didn't want to believe it, I knew he was right.

Ever since I started to communicate, my hope has been drawn time and again towards women like a moth to a flame, only for me to be burned by the scalding chill of their indifference. I've met women who have found me an oddity to be inspected, and others who think I'm a challenge to be overcome. One woman I met through an Internet dating site stared at me as if I was an exhibit at the zoo, while another, who was a speech therapist, gave me a straw when I arrived to see her socially before asking me to blow through it as she would a patient doing a breathing exercise. I longed to tell these women that I'm not a neutered dog with no bark or bite; I have longings and feelings just like they do.

Soon after returning from Israel, I met a woman who captured my attention just as others had done and once again I allowed hope to take root inside me. I told myself the professor was wrong. What did he know? I had confounded expectations in other ways and would do so again. I was sure this woman's interest in me was genuine and my heart soared when we went out one evening to eat pizza and chat. For a few short hours, I felt as normal as everyone else. Then the woman emailed me to let me know that she had a new boyfriend and I felt crushed again.

I was such a fool. How could I hope that a woman might love me? Why would she? I know I bruise too easily and am too quick to feel pain and sadness. It makes me envy people my age who had teenage years in which to be knocked by life and learn to play by its rules. However hard I try not to care, I find it almost impossible to accept that the desire for love that burns so strongly inside me will never be reciprocated.

Now I look out at the sea as I watch waves crashing onto the sand and remember a couple who came to one of the open days I host at the communication centre. I noticed them at once because the man, who arrived with his wife and two small children, was about my age and everything about the couple – from the way they looked at each other to the silences and smiles that communicated so much – told me they were very much in love.

'My husband has a terminal brain tumour and is losing the power of speech,' the woman said to me quietly as her husband looked at some of the equipment we had on show. 'But we want to carry on talking to each other for as long as we can, which is why we came here today to see if you could help.

'He wants to tape video messages for our children while he's still able to and I think he wants to leave one for me as well.'

Suddenly the woman's face froze.

'I'm not ready to let him go yet,' she whispered.

Desolation swept across the woman's face like wind across a deserted winter's beach as she thought of the uncertainty of a future without the man who had anchored her to life.

'Do you think you could help us?' she asked softly.

I nodded at her before she turned to walk back to her husband and I felt grief pierce me. How could a family that loved so much be torn apart? Then another feeling filled me, a kind of envy, because as I looked at the man and woman smile at each other, I realised they'd had the chance to love and be loved that I so fiercely wanted.

Martin giving a presentation at an international conference in Israel

42

Worlds Collide

My mother smiles at the physiotherapist who is pushing me out of her room. I'm sick of coming here week after week, being lifted up and encouraged to take faltering steps on my painful legs and feet. Nevertheless I do it because my parents have never given up the hope of seeing me walk again. I've wondered at times if my family remember the boy I used to be and miss him, which is why they've always wanted me to walk again so badly or to use a computer-generated voice to talk instead of an alphabet board.

It is hard to convince them that my body is unpredictable: just because I can stand up one day, doesn't mean I'll be able to do it the next. It sometimes feels as if I'm almost failing my parents because I don't progress physically in the way they hope I might but I know this is often the case with parents.

When a boy came to the communication centre once to be assessed, we told his mother that he would have to start learning to communicate using a head switch because his neck was the only part of his body he could stabilise. But his mother was adamant: she wanted her son to use his hand not his head. She wanted him to fit in in any way he could, to be as like everyone else as he could in whatever small way.

I understand why my parents want to see me walk and talk but it's exhausting to live in a body that feels like the property of everyone else. That's why I told my mother yesterday that I wanted to have physio only once this week and I'm hoping she'll agree to this compromise.

'Shall we make an appointment for Friday?' the physio asks as my chair comes to rest.

I stare at my mother, willing her to remember what I said.

'Yes,' she says, without looking at me.

The anger I feel burns white hot through my veins. Tomorrow I will go to see my colleague Kitty and rage to her about what has just happened.

'What's the point of communicating if no one listens?!' I'll say. 'Why is it that I talk yet people still refuse to hear what I say even after all these years?'

For now, though, I wrestle back my rage to stop it from dragging everything else down with it. Because, as powerful as it is, the fear I feel about expressing my anger is even stronger. Anger is one of the emotions I still find almost impossible to show because I had to force myself to swallow it for so long. I don't feel I can express it even now, trapped as I am by both the monotone of my computer-generated voice and the constant fear of alienating people. After spending so long as an outsider, I don't want to do anything that might make me one again.

As time passes, I realise that I feel afraid a lot now: I'm

scared of doing the wrong thing, offending someone or not doing a job well enough; I'm fearful of stepping on someone's toes, not being up to what is asked of me or expressing an opinion that will surely be ridiculed. The feeling is almost constant and it's the reason why I don't tell my mother what I really think six years after starting to communicate.

There's another world I inhabit, though. In that world I became one of the first two South Africans with non-functioning speech ever to graduate when I finished my university course and was chosen to meet President Thabo Mbeki. I've travelled, spoken in front of hundreds of people and I'm respected by my colleagues.

But in my personal life, even though my family and friends are my lifeline, I remain in many ways a passive child who is wiped and wheeled, smiled at and sidelined at times, just as I've always been. My parents continue to care for me physically, protecting me from much of the outside world and the harms it might inflict, but I wish they'd listen to me more sometimes. With my sister Kim, I sometimes feel as if I'm a rehabilitation project rather than a brother when she brings home new pieces of equipment from the UK – anti-slip mats for the bathroom or plastic borders to stop food falling off my plate. To others, I'm an occasional charity project, someone who needs to be fixed, or the silent man who sits smiling placidly in a corner. Taken together it makes me feel as if I have no right to life, as if I must always ask permission for fear of doing the wrong thing. The past continues to cast its shadow over me.

I long to rebel but I don't know how. Once I had petty, hidden ways at my disposal and can remember the grim satisfaction that filled me years ago when I watched my leg callipers gouge the paintwork on my mother's car. I was wearing them after a particularly painful operation so I was pleased by my accidental act of rebellion as Mum helped me out of the car.

Today I can't justify such bad behaviour nor can I lay all the blame for my frustration at other people's doors. Even a lion cub won't leave its mother if it's too afraid. I know independence is taken as much as it's given and I must learn to claim mine but sometimes I wonder if I will ever find the courage to do so. It's 2007 and earlier this year, I finally left my job at the communication centre and started working full time at the scientific research institute. It's an excellent promotion – the kind of professional good fortune that many people like me never get the chance to experience.

As everyone at my new workplace is encouraged to study, I applied to do a part-time degree at a university but was told that I had to graduate from high school first. No one would listen, however patiently I tried to explain, that I'd just graduated from another university course as one of the top of the class. The mountain I'd climbed to achieve my qualification meant nothing now that I was applying somewhere different with its own set of rules.

So now I'm studying each night when I get back from work for a high school diploma that sixteen year olds do, and I question if there's any point in trying to move forward in life when the weight of everything holding me back feels too heavy to bear at times. As I consider it all, I wonder if soon I'll feel too afraid, too disbelieving that I have earned a place in life to be able to fight for one any more.

43

Strangers

It was only when I finally gave up on life that I realised we don't need ropes and chains to keep us tethered to this world – even the most insignificant acts can keep us bound to it.

It was 1998 and I was twenty-two years old. I'd started to become aware six long years before and was convinced by then that no one would ever know I was whole inside. After so many years of hoping in vain that I might be rescued, the thought of never escaping the crushing monotony of my existence had made me shut down inside. I just wanted my life to end and nearly got my wish when I became seriously ill with pneumonia.

Finding out that I would have to go to the care home in the country that I hated so much was what made me finally give up. I can remember my parents taking us all to see some friends of theirs. As my mother fed me lunch, I knew there was nothing I could do to show anyone that I didn't want to be sent away again. My family had no idea how desperate I felt inside as they chatted and laughed around me.

The following week I got a runny nose that quickly got worse. People soon realised it wasn't just a cold when my temperature rose and I started vomiting. In fact, I became so ill that my parents took me to the emergency department at the local hospital, where a doctor gave me some medication before sending me home again. When I got worse again, my mother took me back to the hospital and demanded that someone take an X-ray of my chest. They then discovered that I had pneumonia.

I didn't care whether I was treated or not. All I could think about was being sent away when Dad went on his upcoming business trip. I knew I couldn't bear it again. As my kidneys and liver started to shut down, I could hear my parents talking worriedly as they sat beside me and I dipped in and out of consciousness. I knew I was in a room with other patients and sometimes I could hear nurses rushing in to see them when an alarm went off.

Sadness created a chasm inside me. I was tired of living. I didn't want to fight any more. As a mask was slipped over my face so that I could be given oxygen, I prayed for it to be taken off; when a physiotherapist came to pound my ribcage and clear my chest, I hoped she wouldn't be able to; and as she tried feeding a tube down my unwilling throat to relieve the congestion in my chest, I wished she'd leave me alone.

'I've got to get this into you,' she said to me almost angrily. 'You'll die if I don't.'

I rejoiced when I heard those words. I prayed that the infection would overwhelm me and free me from purgatory as it battled for control of my body. I could hear my parents talking about the information file beside my bed that Dad always read whenever he arrived. Kim came to see me too and the sound of the clogs she was wearing echoed through the corridor outside my room, while the brightness of her smile as she looked at me almost cut through the darkness. But nothing reached me and I listened without hearing to nurses complaining about their working conditions or the dates they'd been on with their boyfriends.

'I had a good look at him when he walked into the cinema in front of me,' one said to another as they washed me. 'He's got such a sexy bum.'

'You've got a one-track mind,' her friend admonished with a giggle.

It was as if I was being sucked deeper and deeper down a rabbit hole. I urged my body to give up. I wasn't needed in this world by anyone and no one would notice if I disappeared. I wasn't interested in the future because all I wanted was to die. So hope was like a breath of fresh air blowing through a tomb when it came.

I was lying in bed one afternoon when I heard someone talking to a nurse. Then a face appeared and I realised that it was a woman I knew a little called Myra. She worked in the office where my father got cheques signed in his role as chairman of the management committee for my care centre. But now Myra had come to see me and I didn't understand why because only my family ever visited.

'How are you, Martin?' Myra said as she bent over me. 'I wanted to come and see you because I've heard how ill you've been. You poor boy. I hope they're looking after you well here.'

Myra's face was anxious as she looked down at me. As she smiled hesitantly, I suddenly realised that another human being, unconnected to me by blood or obligation, had thought about me. However much I didn't want it to, that realisation gave me strength. Almost unconsciously after that I began to notice warmth from other people: a nursing sister I overheard telling another that she liked me because I was a good patient, a carer who soothed my aching skin by rubbing lotion into my shoulder to stop me developing a bedsore, and a man who smiled as he walked by while I was sitting in the car on the day I left hospital. All these incidents didn't come together at once but, looking back, I know these tiny gestures from strangers were what started to tether me to the world again.

I was finally roped to it by something that occurred when I got back to my care home. Despite all that had happened to convince me I had a place in the world, disappointment pervaded: I hadn't even been able to die properly. Breath filled my body, I woke up in the morning and fell asleep at night, I was fed food to build up my strength and put out to sit in the sunshine like a plant that needed tending. There was nothing I could do to stop people from keeping me alive.

But as I lay on a bean-bag one day, a carer sat down beside me. She was new so I didn't really know her but I recognised her voice as she spoke to me. Her hands took hold of one of my feet as she started to massage it and I felt her pummel my aching and ugly foot with her hands, soothing out the knots and relaxing away the tension. I couldn't believe that she wanted to touch me and the fact that she did made me realise that maybe there was some tiny reason not to give up on life completely. Perhaps I wasn't as repulsive as I believed I was.

Then I heard the familiar crunch of the zipped pencil bag the woman always carried around with her, which was full of the oils she used for aromatherapy. 'There, now,' she said softly as the smell of mint pierced the air. 'I'm sure that feels much better, doesn't it? Why don't we do your other foot and see if we can relax that a bit too?'

The woman's name, of course, was Virna and it was the first time she'd really spoken to me. But that moment was the one that drew all the other pieces together and made the jigsaw whole. I didn't know what each of those strangers had given me until one of them touched my broken, twisted, useless body and made me realise that I wasn't completely abhorrent. And it was then that I realised that families might be the ones who pick us up time and again but strangers can also rescue us – even if they don't know they're doing so.

44

Everything Changes

I know a life can be destroyed in an instant: a car spins out of control on a busy road, a doctor sits down to break bad news or a love letter is discovered hidden in a place where its owner thought it never would be found. All these things can shatter a world in just a few moments. But is it possible for the opposite to happen – for a life to be created in a moment instead of destroyed? For a man to see a face and know it belongs to the woman he will spend the rest of his life with?

She is the kind of woman who would make any man's heart sing and yet I feel sure there is something about her that speaks to me alone. I met her on New Year's Day a month ago when Kim called from England. I didn't pay much attention at first as my parents chatted to my sister via webcam and I heard her introducing them to the friends she was spending the day with. But then I turned my head, saw a woman with blue eyes, blonde hair and the warmest smile I'd ever seen and my world shifted forever.

She was sitting between Kim and a third woman with dark brown hair. They giggled together as their faces squeezed onto the screen.

'This is Danielle,' Kim said, gesturing to the dark-haired woman. 'And this is Joanna.'

'Hi Martin,' they said in unison.

I could hear immediately that they were both South African. She smiled. I smiled back.

'Ooh!' said Danielle. 'He's handsome.'

My face burned crimson as the three of them laughed together before Kim got up to go and do something and I was left alone with Joanna and Danielle.

'Show us your arms!' Danielle said. 'I'm an occupational therapist so I know guys like you usually have great arms!'

I felt my face burn even redder as I looked at them. I wasn't sure what to say.

'How are you both?' I wrote.

'Good!' Danielle said. 'What are you doing today?'

'Working, like every other day. How was your New Year's Eve?'

'Fun. We went into London. It was great.'

Joanna was quieter than Danielle but I watched her eyes slide downwards whenever I wrote something. She was listening to every word I said. I wanted to hear her speak.

'So how do you know my sister, Joanna?' I asked.

'We work together,' she said. 'I'm a social worker like Kim.'

'How long have you been in the UK?'

'Seven years.'

'And do you like it?'

'Yes. I work too hard but I enjoy it.'

She smiled and the two of us started talking. It was nothing out of the ordinary. We just chatted about our Christmases and the resolutions we were making for the New Year, music we liked and films we wanted to see. But as Danielle drifted away from the computer and we carried on talking, the words hardly seemed to matter. Joanna was beautiful, so beautiful, and easy to chat to: she laughed and made jokes, listened to what I said and asked me questions. It was unusual for me to find someone I could talk with so easily and two hours slid by in a blur.

'I have to go,' I said reluctantly when I realised that it was well past midnight.

'But why?' Joanna asked. 'Aren't you enjoying talking?'

I longed to tell her how much.

'I've got an early start tomorrow,' I said, not wanting to say that my father needed to put me to bed because it was late and he wanted to sleep.

'Okay,' Joanna replied. 'Shall we be Facebook friends so that we can talk some more?'

'Yes. Let's speak again soon.'

We said goodbye and excitement buzzed inside me as I shut down the computer and took Kojak outside for his final run of the night. Joanna was so friendly. She seemed interested in me and obviously wanted to talk more.

But then reality hit again. Just before Christmas I'd met a woman I'd liked very much and was pleased when she invited me to the theatre. Then she arrived with her boyfriend and I felt like a particularly pathetic kind of dog that was being given a treat. Why was I letting myself get excited again now?

It had been proven to me over and over again that I wasn't the kind of man women wanted to love and I'd been rejected too many times. If Joanna wanted friendship from me – just like every other woman I met – then I would have to content myself with that.

As I went inside and got into bed, I made a promise to forget what had happened. Joanna was a world away from me and it would stay that way. I was being foolish, wishing for something I'd been shown time and again was impossible for me to have.

Then an email arrived.

'Hi Martin,' Joanna wrote. 'I was waiting for a message from you but didn't get one so I thought I'd contact you instead. I enjoyed talking to you so let me know if you want to chat some more.'

What could I do? No man could resist such temptation.

45

Meeting Mickey?

'I have something to ask you,' Joanna says as I look at her face on the screen.

It is the middle of February and we've been in constant contact since we met. For the first week or so we sent polite emails, edging our way forwards together like swimmers dipping their toes into the sea before deciding to dive in. But we soon forgot our caution and started talking every evening over the Internet. Each night was as easy as the first and we once found ourselves chatting online as dawn broke before realising there was still more to say.

I've never known it could be like this with another person – so easy and simple – or that talking to a woman could feel as natural as it does with Joanna. I want to know everything about her and words tumble out of us as we tell each other about our lives and what has happened in them – from tiny, insignificant details like the songs we love to the most important events of my life as a ghost boy and the death of Joanna's father, whom she adored. It is as if there is nothing I can't say because Joanna listens in a way I've never known before: she is interested, funny and sensitive, positive, enquiring and a dreamer just like me. We talk about the tiny details of our days and our hopes for the future, we joke together and laugh, and talk more honestly about our innermost feelings than I've ever done before. There is no need to hide.

I feel I can trust her. Every time she smiles, my resolve to keep my feelings in perspective weakens a little more and reason is forgotten as I feel myself plunging ever more deeply into this new world. At thirty-three, Joanna is a year older than me. She is a social worker like my sister Kim and lives near her in Essex. But the link with Kim is just the last in a long line of almost meetings we've had over the years. Joanna and I realised that we attended the same regional sports event when we were schoolchildren and she even visited my care home when she was a student. We have come so close to meeting so many times it seems inevitable we finally did. If I believed in fate, I'd think we were destined to meet.

Joanna looks a little nervous now as she opens her mouth to speak and I smile to myself. Even after such a short time, I know her face well enough to know if she is tired or happy, annoyed or exasperated. I've spent hour after hour studying her as we talk and I've realised that her face is not a mask like some people's – instead every emotion can be found written on it if I look hard enough.

'I'm going to Disney World on holiday later this month,' she says, the words coming out in a rush. 'And I've been thinking about this all night so I'm just going to say it: will you come with me? I know it's soon but it just seems right somehow.'

I stare at the screen in disbelief. Happiness fills me with every syllable she speaks.

'I know you haven't flown long haul before but I'm sure we could find an airline that would take you,' she says. 'I've looked at tickets and there are seats available.

'I'm going for two weeks but you could stay as long as you want. I've contacted the hotel I'm booked into and the room I'll be staying in has two beds so we can share it. Please think about what I'm saying. Don't just say no.

'I want to meet you and I think you want to meet me too. Please don't let money be the issue or worry too much about work. I understand you might feel you can't just leave things but sometimes in life you have to, don't you think?'

My hand freezes above the keyboard. What almost surprises me most is that I'm not afraid or uncertain. I feel overwhelmed but I'm ecstatic, not fearful. She wants to meet me. I don't need to ask myself if I want to go. I want to meet Joanna more than I've ever wanted anything in my life. But as I wonder how I will tell her this, I realise that words will never be enough.

'I'd love to come,' I type. 'I really would.'

'Really?'

She smiles and waits for me to say something more but I can't. My mind is whirring as I look at her on the computer screen in front of me.

'I know you'll need some help and I don't mind doing

that,' she says. 'It's just that we have this chance to meet and I think we should grab it!'

She giggles. I love it when she laughs.

'Why do you want to meet me?' I say.

I have to ask. The question has been running around my head ever since she first asked me to take part in this crazy plan.

She is silent for a moment.

'Because you're the most honest man I've ever met,' she says. 'And because, although I've only known you for a few weeks, you've made me so happy. You make me laugh, you're interesting and you understand what I say in a way no one else ever has before.'

We are silent for a moment. I can see her on the webcam as she lifts her hand towards the screen and I know she is reaching out to touch me from 6,000 miles away.

'So you're definitely going to come?' she asks.

'I want to,' I say. 'I will do all that I can to meet you.'

I look at her face. I can hardly believe she is so sure of life that she believes it can be as simple as buying a plane ticket and meeting a stranger. She is so certain that we will both find love one day and tells me we can't hurry or control it, we must just let it unfold as it wants to. She doesn't feel defeated by love as I do at times and I can feel her optimism infecting me cell by cell, making me believe that anything is possible.

'Things happen at the right time,' Joanna tells me. 'There's a plan for each one of us.'

I raise my hand to cover hers on the screen in front of me. How I long to feel Joanna close to me; how my heart turns when I look at her face and realise she really means what she says. She wants to meet me. She wants to spend time getting to know me. I can't wait to know her. But first there is something I must talk to her about.

'I want to tell you about myself physically,' I write. 'I want you to understand exactly who I am.'

'Okay,' she says.

46

The Real Me

'I'm not going to sugar-coat it,' I write to her in an email. 'I'm going to tell you everything I need help with and if you change your mind after reading it, that's fine.

'I eat everything and can feed myself finger food but I need help with a knife and fork. I can't get in and out of the shower alone but I can wash and dry myself, although I might ask you to unscrew the shampoo lid.

'I also need to be shaved because I can't do it myself and I can pretty much dress myself if my clothes are laid out next to me. I can't do up buttons, zips or shoelaces though.

'I need help getting on and off the toilet and in and out of cars from my wheelchair. I can't sit up unsupported so I need to be leaned against something if I'm not in my chair.

'I can use my feet to move my wheelchair around on floorboards but not on carpeted floors and while I can move my chair by pushing off from surfaces with my arms, I'm not strong enough to push myself along a road or pavement if I'm in my manual chair.

'I think that's basically it. Oh, and I drink with a straw.'

I stare at the screen one last time. My heartbeat quickens as I hit the send button. I wonder if I'm mad to spell this out so bleakly in black and white. But I want to be completely honest with Joanna because I don't need a carer or someone who pities me. I don't want a dreamer whose fantasy will crumble when reality hits, someone who wants to rescue me or a woman who loves me in spite of my less than perfect body. If I want to be loved for who I am, then Joanna must know all of me. Even though I'm afraid of telling her this, I somehow feel sure she won't care. I can't explain exactly why. I just know she won't.

The next morning I receive a reply to my message.

'None of it matters,' Joanna writes. 'We can work it out as we go along.'

The feeling inside me is like the peace that comes when the final leaf falls from a tree in an autumn wood. Everything is quiet. I've lived my whole life as a burden. She makes me feel weightless.

47

A Lion's Heart

How did Joanna come to be so fearless? I've asked myself this again and again in the days since she left for America alone because I couldn't get a visa in time to meet her there. We were both bitterly disappointed but at least we know now that it is only a question of when, not if, we will meet.

For now, I'm learning to negotiate my way around the edges of the unexpected new shape my life is taking on. Until now my existence has been full of the straight corners and neat edges that come with order and routine. But suddenly it is full of unexpected curves and the kind of chaos that I'm learning another person can create. Joanna is uprooting everything I trained myself to expect and accept: I'd resigned myself to leading a serious life full of work and study, yet suddenly she makes me laugh until I cry; I believed I would never find a woman to love and now I'm beginning to hope that I have. I'm usually so careful and considered but Joanna is making me reckless. She doesn't see barriers but possibilities; she is utterly unafraid and I'm beginning to feel that way too.

She told me it was a childhood friend of hers who taught her to look beyond a person's body after he was paralysed from the neck down. He was only in his twenties and might have thought his life had no meaning after the night when the car he was travelling in was hit by a train. Instead, he determined to become a farmer like his father. Today he is married and runs a 1,000-acre farm.

'He might not be able to drink tea on his own but he can manage a farm because he can speak and that's all he needs,' Joanna told me. 'He's also far happier than most people I know.'

But I believe the roots of her fearlessness stretch further back to her childhood in the South African countryside when the freedom that is so much a part of the land there seeped into her. And if there is one person responsible for her courage, I think it is her father, At Van Wyk. He was also a farmer and from the moment his three daughters and son were old enough to look after themselves he let them loose on his land.

'You should always try things until you can't do them any more,' he used to tell his children, 'rather than say no and not try at all.'

So Joanna and her siblings learned to handle guns safely when they were still young and roamed free around the land their father farmed. When At had a heart attack at the age of thirty-six, one of the first things he did after coming out of hospital following a bypass operation was to throw a loop of rope over the highest tree branch he could find and hoist up a swing for his children. It hung far above a dry riverbed.

'How high can you go?' he called in delight as they soared through the air above him.

At knew he'd come close to death decades earlier than he should have but he wasn't going to be intimidated into being overly cautious about himself or his children. So when he took them to the coast to see the sea, he'd let them swim into the waves, always keeping an eye on them to make sure they were safe but letting them test the water and themselves. When they went into the bush to spot game, he'd let Joanna, her sisters and brother sit in the back of an open-top truck.

'I'll stop and pick them up when they fall out but not before then,' he told the mother of one of Joanna's friends when she objected to how the children were going to travel.

Joanna's most treasured memories are of the holidays she and her family took each year to a farm on the edge of the Kruger National Park that belonged to her father's best friend. For those precious weeks Joanna and her siblings would roam the bush, searching for lions, wildebeest, elephants and impala as they learned valuable lessons about the wildlife and themselves.

First, came the humility of understanding how little human wishes really matter: elephants treading their familiar paths to water will trample over people if their route is blocked, and a swarm of bees won't stand for a thieving finger that wants a taste of honey. However important we each think we are, we are but a footnote to the natural cycle.

Secondly, they learned to be aware every moment after discovering that lions become almost invisible when they lie down in long, arid bush grass to sleep each afternoon. The children had to be constantly vigilant, watching every step they made, to avoid inadvertently stumbling upon a sleeping pride.

And finally, they learned the art of bravery and how to apply it: faced with an angry elephant, they knew they had to run as fast as possible but if a lion charged at them, they must fool the cat into thinking they weren't prey worth having by staying rooted to the spot.

These were the lessons Joanna learned as a child and this fearlessness gave her a freedom of spirit that I'd never known existed until now. But bit by bit she is beginning to pass it on to me and I feel as if I am beginning to soar inside.

48

I Tell Her

Late last night I wrote to her: 'I can't stop thinking about you. I love you. I had to tell you.'

How do I know this? I can't say for sure but something other than logic and reason tells me it's true. I've known her for only a few weeks, yet I'm sure I will know her for a lifetime now.

'My love,' Joanna writes the next morning. 'Do you know how long I've wanted to start a letter with those words? But until now there has never been an opportunity for me to do it. How happy you make me. I love you so much it's almost painful.'

My heart turns over when I read those words.

'I know it's crazy because we haven't even met yet,' I write. 'But I'm more sure of you than I've been of anything before.'

'I understand,' she tells me. 'I have to keep reminding myself this is real because sometimes I can't quite believe I feel this way. How can I? I never knew I could have feelings like this and it makes me almost afraid. It's as if I don't have control over my emotions any more.'

'But however many times I ask myself if I'm mad, I know that I don't care,' I tell her. 'I love you. It's as simple as that.'

We talk urgently, words flying back and forth on emails, text messages and down Internet phone lines, as we try to make sense of what we are experiencing.

'But how can you be sure of how you feel when we haven't met?' Joanna asks.

'Because I can feel it physically, within every fibre,' I tell her. 'My heart contracts when I say the words to you. I know it doesn't make sense on so many levels but it's as though we're connected. I feel more accepted by you than anyone I've ever met before.'

'I feel almost mad,' she writes. 'It's as if I have to stop and pinch myself sometimes because I'm totally in love with a man I haven't even met and yet I feel as if I've known you for years.'

I understand why we must ask questions about a hurricane that has stormed into both of our lives without warning. It is disorienting when your world becomes a different place almost overnight. But love isn't about logic and our phantom doubts are easily dismissed. Over the years, I'd often heard people say that you know when you meet the right person and now I understand what they meant. The feeling is unlike anything I've ever known.

49

Sugar and Salt

I'm losing myself in Joanna as we dream together.

'I want to dance with you,' I tell her.

We paint pictures with words as we tell each other about all the things we'll do when we finally meet. We are online almost constantly now when we aren't at work. Our days have fallen into a rhythm that we share from opposite sides of the world because the time difference between South Africa and England is only a couple of hours. It means I can wake Joanna up in the morning with a text, chat to her before we go to work and email throughout the day before spending all evening online together. We don't turn our computers off even when one of us needs to eat or answer a telephone call. If Joanna calls me last thing at night, I speak to her using beeps on my phone for 'No' and 'Yes' so we can say a final few words to each other.

Our longing for each other is so strong that I recently decided to text her after waking up in the early hours of the morning, knowing that she would be on her way home from a night out with friends.

'You've just woken me up,' I joked and seconds later my phone beeped.

'You're not going to believe this,' Joanna messaged back. 'But I just dropped my keys as I was unlocking the door and thought I must have woken you up before realising that I couldn't possibly have.'

Another day my right hand started to hurt and I told Joanna I didn't understand why it was painful.

'I hurt my right hand today too!' she said as she laughed.

I can't explain these things but I don't need to question mysterious coincidences when I can concentrate on what is real. It is April 2008 and I've booked a flight to go to the UK at the beginning of June. It's just eight weeks until Joanna and I will be together and we can decide what will happen next for us. We already know that we love each other, which means we have no choice but to find a way to be together.

My parents are quietly agitated. Will the airline agree to let me fly so far alone? Who will feed me from the tiny plate of food that I will be given or hold me in my seat to make sure I don't hit my head when gravity thrusts me forward as we land because I don't have enough balance to resist it? But even as their questions buzz in the air around me, I remind myself of the promise I made to gain my independence. I am thirty-two years old. It's been almost seven years since I was first assessed and I've learned so much. It's time now. I don't have to be afraid any longer.

However sure Joanna and I are, though, we know we must learn to steer our relationship through the rocks of other

people's misgivings if it is to survive. As the weeks have
turned into months, it's become more and more clear that
some suspect our feelings are a fiction we are writing together
without the inconvenience of mundane reality to ruin our
plot. They think the illusion won't be sustained by real life and
I can understand their scepticism: we've never met, our lives
are completely different and this doesn't make any sense. But
there are also times when I wish that Joanna didn't have to
experience the pain of other people's good intentions. Even
though I'm well used to it, I'd do anything to protect her from
its bite.

'What's happened?' I asked her one evening.

Her face was flatter than usual, the light drained out of it.

'I've had a terrible afternoon,' she said.

'Why?'

'I saw some friends and was so excited to talk to them
about you. But they just didn't want to listen. All they kept
asking was whether I realised how vulnerable you must be.
They thought I was being cruel to make you believe we might
have a future together.'

Her voice cracked with sadness.

'It was awful,' she told me. 'I couldn't say anything
because I didn't trust myself to speak.'

'I'm so sorry.'

'It's not your fault. But I don't understand how my friends
could even say such things to me. Don't they know me at all?
It's as if I'm a child they don't trust.'

'I know the feeling well.'

Her face lightened for a moment before becoming sad
again.

'It makes me wonder what other people will think when they meet us,' she says. 'It upsets me to realise that all they might see is your chair. It's so wrong. My friends didn't even mention the fact that we hadn't met yet. All they were worried about was what matters the least.'

'It often happens that way,' I wrote. 'People forget everything except the fact that I can't walk.'

'I know,' she said sadly. 'But it shouldn't be that way.'

As I watched Joanna talk, I was filled with the desire to reach out and touch her, physically reassure her that we will prove people wrong. I wished I had some way to show her how sure I am that we will. Love is another form of faith, after all. I know ours is real and I believe in it completely.

'People will have to learn to deal with us because this is how we feel and we can't change it,' I told her.

'But do you think they will?'

'Yes.'

She was silent for a moment.

'It just makes me feel sad to know that I won't be able to discuss you with my friends again. It feels as if I'll never be able to trust them with the most precious thing in my life.'

'Maybe in time you will. They might change their minds when they see that we're staying together whatever happens.'

She smiled at me.

'Maybe, my liefie,' she said softly.

That is my name now: my liefie, my love.

We face obstacles, for sure. Being on different continents and talking solely via the phone and Internet, instead of face to face, can easily give rise to misunderstandings so we've started to make rules. The first is that we must always be honest with each other; the next is that we'll solve problems together.

'You've got to eat a little salt,' South African mothers say to their children as they try to teach them that nothing is perfect when they come home crying about a playground injustice.

Joanna and I know this and the setbacks we are experiencing – whether it's other people's questions or the reluctance of the airline authorities to fly me to the UK – are bringing us closer together. To get booked on a flight to London, I've needed medical clearance and permissions, forms filled out and notes written by doctors. But Joanna has been as determined as I am that we won't be beaten. It felt like we'd taken on the world and won when she called me at work one morning.

'The airline has agreed to fly you,' I heard her say. 'You're coming to the UK.'

It was a huge victory for us but there are other smaller troubles that we are also learning to overcome together.

'I've realised that I'll never hear you say my name,' Joanna told me one night.

We'd never spoken about it before but I could hear the pain in her voice as she talked to me.

'It makes me feel so sad to know that I'll never hear the words "I love you",' she said. 'And although I have no idea why I'm thinking about this, for some reason I can't stop now. It's as if I've lost something even though I'm not sure what it is.'

I longed to comfort her but didn't know how to at first. I take my silence almost for granted after so many years and long ago stopped grieving for a voice that I don't even remember having but I understood that Joanna was mourning something precious. A few days later we were talking online as I started to hit the keys on my laptop to activate my communication system. I rarely use it to speak to Joanna because my hands are strong enough now for me to type while we talk and my laptop isn't compatible with our Internet phone line. But ever since she'd spoken about wanting to hear my voice, I'd been working on something for her.

'Listen,' I wrote. 'There is something that I want to say.'

She fell silent as I hit a final key on the laptop keyboard in front of me.

'Joanna,' a voice said.

It was Perfect Paul and he pronounced Joanna's name just as I'd taught him to after spending hours unravelling his vowel and consonant pronunciation. Instead of saying it in the English way – Jo-A-nA – Perfect Paul had pronounced it with an Afrikaans inflection, just as she is used to hearing – Jo-nAH.

'I love you,' Perfect Paul said.

Joanna smiled before laughing.

'Thank you.'

Recently I sent her an envelope containing a photocopy of my hands after she told me again and again how much she longed to touch them.

'Now I have you with me,' she said with a smile from a world away.

It's true there is salt as well as sweet in every life. I hope we'll always share both.

50

Falling

It's right to say that people fall in love. We don't glide, slip or stumble into it. Instead we tumble head first from the moment we decide to step off the edge of a cliff with someone and see whether we'll fly together. Love might be irrational but we make the choice to risk everything. I know I'm taking a gamble with Joanna because there will always be a fraction of doubt, however tiny, until we meet. The greatest lesson I'm learning with her, though, is that living life is about taking chances, even if they make you feel afraid.

It was about a week after we met that I made the choice to allow myself to fall in love with Joanna. She'd sent me an email and I was just about to reply when I suddenly stopped myself.

'Am I going to take another chance with my heart?' I thought. 'Am I going to gamble again?'

I knew the answer to my question as soon as I'd asked it because the prize at stake was the one I wanted most, after all.

I knew what I had to do. But I promised myself that if I was going to find a real love, one that could weather the inevitable storms a lifetime together would bring, I mustn't pretend to be what I wasn't. I wanted to be completely honest with Joanna about whatever we discussed – whether it was the abuse I'd suffered, my care needs or the longing I had to make love to a woman – because I couldn't let fear force me to hide myself.

Sometimes I felt brave when I told her things, at others my terror of rejection was the spectre that stalked me, but I forced myself to continue. Everything I've learned since the day I was wheeled into a room and asked to focus my eyes on a picture of a ball has made me able to now risk my heart. The lessons had been painful at times but being out in the world, making mistakes and progressing has taught me that life can't be experienced at arm's length like an academic project. It must be lived and for too long I've tried to keep it at bay by burying myself in work and study.

I understand now why it happened. For a long time I didn't know how to be in the world. I found it confusing, disorienting, and in many ways I was like a child. I believed back then that good and bad were black and white just as I'd seen on the television for so many years, and I spoke the truth exactly as I saw it. But I quickly learned that people don't always want to hear the truth. What might seem like the right thing isn't always necessarily so. It was hard, though, because most of what I had to learn was unseen and unspoken.

The most difficult thing to master was the complex web of manners and hierarchies my colleagues navigated. I knew that understanding these rules would help me in so many ways but

I was too scared even to try at first for fear of making a mistake. Instead of speaking up at meetings and using some of the words I'd spent hours inputting onto my computer just in case I needed them, I stayed silent. And rather than talk openly to colleagues I didn't know well, I was quiet. When one told me she was just 'babysitting' me, I stared at her blankly because I wasn't sure what to say.

But gradually I've learned to trust my own judgement – even if it is sometimes wrong – as I've realised that life is about shades of grey, instead of black and white. And the most important thing I've learned is how to take risks because I'd never taken them before I started to communicate. But I was forced to after I started working because I knew I'd never move up the career ladder if I didn't. So I put in hours of extra time, kept quiet when I was given tasks I didn't understand and crushed my disappointment when colleagues were praised for work I felt I'd contributed towards. On the other hand, I met so many people who helped and guided me, listened and bolstered me when I doubted myself.

It is impossible to underestimate how hard I found it at times to believe in myself. When I was sitting trying to solve a complex computer problem, ghosts from all the years of being treated as an imbecile would haunt me. It wasn't until I started work that I realised how deeply the need for familiarity and routine had been drilled into me by my years in institutions. All I wanted was to keep moving forward but I felt lost at times, mired in self-doubt, and I found it impossible to relax.

Perhaps this love of routine was why I found it hard to leave jobs behind once I had them – whether it was the health centre, where I got my first job doing filing and photocopying, or the communication centre, where I was given a chance to stretch myself. I felt safe in each place and it was difficult to relinquish that.

While moving to a full-time job at the scientific research institute where I work today was unnerving in many ways, it also forced me to get used to freedom because suddenly I was in an environment where my workload could change unpredictably or deadlines alter without warning. I found it overwhelming at first to be surrounded by people with qualifications, education and experience, when I'd taught myself to read and write at the age of twenty-eight and learned most of what I knew about computers sitting alone at my desk. I felt sure I couldn't keep up with my colleagues, let alone compete with them.

But gradually I realised that it doesn't matter how you reach a place, as long as you deserve to be there. As time has passed, my confidence has grown and I've realised that I'm trusted by my colleagues. It didn't matter that I was self-taught because living life is about checks and balances, small victories and minor failures. I'd spent years longing for things to happen to me, for events to take my life somewhere unexpected. Although I found it disorienting when it started to happen each day, week or month, I learned that this is what life is like – unpredictable, uncontrollable and exciting.

I was still removed from it in many ways because I'd never had the chance to know someone completely, to connect with them in the way that you can do only when you fall in love. Then I met Joanna and now I'm prepared to take the greatest chance with her. For the first time in my life, I don't care what others think or worry about keeping up appearances and creating a good impression. I don't care about letting someone down or not doing a good enough job. I've been trying to justify myself ever since I started to communicate through work and study, learning and achieving. But the one thing I will not justify is Joanna.

Recently I told her that I wanted her to see exactly what I looked like before I arrived in England. Sitting in front of the computer, I held a web camera in my right hand, which I guided back and forth. First I showed her my face, then my arms and the loose cotton T-shirt covering my chest before pulling the camera back so that she could see the chair I sit in each and every day. She'd seen it before, of course, but now I trained the camera on myself and showed her every detail so that nothing was hidden. Joanna laughed softly as I pointed the camera at the metal plates that supported my bare feet.

'Hobbit toes!' she said with a giggle.

But even as I searched her face on the screen in front of me for signs of fear or confusion, I knew I wouldn't find them. After a lifetime of such looks, I can recognise them in an instant but there was nothing on Joanna's face except a smile.

'You're beautiful,' she said softly.

It is her belief in me that tells me I'm right to risk everything for her.

51

Climbing

I stare at the sand dune above me. It shimmers in the heat.

'Are you ready?' my brother David asks.

I nod.

We're on holiday in Namibia. My mother was born here and we have come to see the country where she grew up after Kim arrived on a trip from the UK. I look at the dune and wonder how I'm ever going to get up it: it is more than a hundred metres high. Mum and Dad have gone off to explore and I've told David that I want to reach the top of the dune. Surprise flitted across his face before he got out of the car, unloaded my chair from the boot and helped me into it before pushing me through the sand. Now I look up at the dune rising above me. I want to get Joanna some sand from the top of it. This dune is one of the highest in the world and the desert is one of her favourite places.

'The silence is so complete that you don't realise you've never heard anything like it until you're there,' she told me.

'And the landscape is so huge that it changes with every hour of the day. Even the sand is softer than anything you've touched before.'

That's why I want to bottle some sand from the top of the dune for her and send it back to the UK with Kim as a reminder of me and the trips she once made to the desert with her family. Heat shimmers in waves as I look up at people running down the dune after reaching the top. They are laughing and shrieking as they hurtle down after the long climb.

'How are we going to do this?' my brother asks.

I'm not sure. David takes me under the right arm and helps me to stand up before I drop onto my knees in the sand. I can't crawl so my brother pulls me forward as I try to help by digging my other arm into the sand to propel myself too. Slowly we start to move up the dune as people walking back down to cool drinks and shade stare at us in surprise. It's almost midday, too late to be doing something like this. The sand is so warm and soft by now that it keeps collapsing and I must dig myself out before carrying on upwards. We should have come at dawn when the sand was cooler and firmer.

The sun beats down as David hauls me upwards. We both begin to sweat as we climb – he pulling, me digging my elbow into the sand and pushing against it to try and take some of the load of my dead weight from my brother. Higher and higher we climb, me wriggling in the sand and David pulling me upwards. The dune gets steeper the nearer to the top we get.

'Do you really want to get all the way up there?' David asks as we stop to rest.

He stares upwards and my eyes follow his. I have to get to the summit. Like a tribesman superstitiously dancing for rain,

I must convince the heavens to smile on me and prove to Joanna that there is no barrier I will not overcome for her — even my own body. This will be the final proof that she is a part of me now and I must show her that she will make me more than I ever thought I could be.

David sighs in exasperation as I smile at him and we start edging our way up again, metre by metre. There is sand in our hair, mouths and eyes, and the light bouncing off the dune is blinding.

'Don't stop!' a voice calls. 'You're so nearly there.'

I look down. Kim is walking up to join us. Far below, I can see our parents standing by the car and staring up at the three of us. They wave as I look down.

'Let's go,' David says.

We've been climbing for about forty-five minutes now and the people who started the journey with us have long since walked back down to earth. We must make one final effort to get to the top of the dune. It is so close now. I think of Joanna once more as I dig into the sand and push myself upwards. Bit by bit I scrabble towards the summit. The sky is azure blue above me and my mouth is dry. My heart beats with exertion and I can hear David panting as he gives my body one final heave. Suddenly we stop to rest.

We are at the top of the sand mountain and Kim sits down beside us. No one speaks as we struggle to get our breath back. Beneath us, the desert spreads out like an endless sea. Kim leans towards me. In her hand is a glass bottle. I watch as she opens it before handing it to me. I push it into the sand.

52

The Ticket

Is it anger or frustration that bites most bitterly at the back of my throat as I stare at the computer screen? It's ten days before I'm due to fly to the UK and I'm at work. I've just received an email from a travel agent I contacted to ask for a quote for flights to Canada. I'm attending a conference there in three months and have asked Joanna to accompany me to the event instead of my mother and father, who have always assisted me in the past. The travel agent is wondering whether I want to go to Canada with my mother or my girlfriend? Apparently Mum picked up the phone when he called to give me some information and told him she was going to book the flights. I know what she's thinking.

'Kim had a friend who met someone on the Internet and thought she was completely in love with him,' Mum said a few nights ago. 'But then she met the man and realised they had nothing in common. It happens a lot, so I hear.'

I'm unsure for a moment how to convince my mother I

know what I'm doing. It's like trying to tell someone who is colour blind that the sky is blue when they are sure it's green.

'Joanna and I know each other too well for that to happen,' I sign to her on my alphabet board. 'We are sure of how we feel. Everything will be fine when we meet.'

Mum sighs.

'I hope so for your sake, Martin,' she says. 'I really do.'

I understand her fear. Her child is spreading his wings two decades after he was supposed to. She has waited a long time for this moment and it frightens her now it has come. I've been suspended in almost childhood all my life: first as a ghost boy and then in recent years as my parents have been involved in every step of my progress. It's hard for them to think of me flying halfway across the world without them and I understand because I'm apprehensive too.

I've only been on one short domestic flight on my own; now I'll have to cross oceans alone to see Joanna and there are so many practical considerations to take into account. I know all my parents want is to keep me safe but I also know I can't spend the rest of my life easing myself away from their expectations and fears. At some point I will have to leap into the unknown without them.

'My love?'

A message from Joanna pops up on my screen. I texted her a few minutes ago to tell her that I needed to talk.

'Thank goodness you're here,' I type back. 'I have something to tell you.'

I explain to her what my mother has done and the worry I have about dissuading her from doing what she believes is for the best.

'But why is your mother involved at all?' Joanna writes when I've finished explaining.

'Because she found out that I was going to book the flights and says she is worried the prices will go up if I don't get the tickets soon,' I reply.

I don't need to say Mum is also worried Joanna and I will break up during my visit to the UK, which will leave me with a useless plane ticket.

'But can't you stop her?' Joanna types. 'Tell her that we're organising it together?'

'I'll try, but I'm not sure she'll listen.'

'She'll have to!'

My screen goes blank for a minute.

'I'm getting angry,' Joanna eventually writes. 'I don't understand why your mother is involved in this at all. Isn't it up to you? If you need help with anything, then I can do it.'

I wish I could explain it to her, make her see that it's not so simple. We have always understood each other until now but suddenly I wonder if this will be the first time we won't be able to.

'This all makes me so angry,' she types. 'Why can't you just tell her not to interfere?'

It's the closest we've ever come to an argument and I feel afraid. How can I explain myself to the girl who roamed the bush and swam in deep water? How do I make her understand when our experiences of life have been so very different?

'My parents are the ones who get me out of bed in the morning,' I write. 'And they are also the ones who help me to dress, feed me my breakfast and wash me, drive me to work and pick me up again.

'What would I do if I made them so angry that they didn't want to do all of those things? I know it wouldn't happen, of course, because they love me and would never do anything to hurt me.

'But knowing something doesn't always mean you aren't afraid of it and being in a wheelchair means that you need people in so many ways that those who aren't don't.'

My screen is blank for a moment. Then five words pop up on the screen from Joanna: 'I am sorry, my love.'

We agree to speak tonight but first I want to talk to my father, so I email him to ask if he will speak to my mother on my behalf. Nothing is said, though, until I sit down with my parents after supper.

'I need to talk to you both,' I say, using my alphabet board. 'It's important.'

My parents look at me. My heart pummels my chest. I have to be direct with them if I'm ever going to make them see how important this is to me.

'I'm going to go to Canada with Joanna,' I say. 'She is going to assist me on this trip because I want her to.'

My mother looks as if she might say something and I pray that she will be silent long enough to let me finish speaking.

'I know you don't think it's a good idea but it's time you started trusting me,' I tell them. 'I have to be able to make my own decisions and mistakes. You can't protect me forever and I'm more sure than I've been of anything before that Joanna and I will make this work.'

My mother is silent for a moment.

'We don't want to stop you from doing anything, Martin,' she says. 'All we want is your happiness.'

'I know,' I tell her. 'But if that's really what you want, then you must give me the chance to find out what my happiness is. Please let me have it. Please let me do this.'

My parents are silent for a moment before my mother gets up.

'I'm going to make more coffee,' she says quietly.

Neither my mother nor my father says anything else. There are so many things my parents leave unsaid. I can only hope that this time they will listen to me.

53

Coming Home

My heart felt as if it was going to stop beating a thousand times after the pilot announced we were flying over Paris. Now I almost wish it had, as a man pushes me through Heathrow airport. Joanna is just a few moments away on the other side of a wall somewhere in this vast building. I try to breathe smoothly but can't. Will the Technicolor world we've lived in for the past six months be dulled to shades of grey when we finally meet?

'Nearly there, sir,' I hear a voice say.

I wonder if this could be a dress rehearsal. Will a director shout 'Cut' so I can go back over my lines one final time? In fact, what are my lines? What am I going to say? My mind has gone blank.

The flight was like an assault course that I had to master stage by stage: get home from the office and pick up my bag; get to the airport and check in; get on the flight and fly for eleven hours without eating or drinking to make sure I didn't spill anything down myself and arrive looking untidy to meet Joanna. But just as I thought I'd got over all the hurdles, a stern-looking official came onto the plane after we had touched down.

'Where are you going?' he asked.

Joanna and I had talked again and again about what kind of questions I might be asked and I'd prepared a special communication board for the flight. But the answer to this question wasn't on it and the man looked annoyed as he waited for me to say something.

'Where is your connecting flight taking you?' he asked.

I stared at him.

'What is your final destination?'

He sighed in frustration at my silence before finally asking me a question I could answer.

'Is London your final stop?'

I nodded and he gestured to an older man.

'He's all yours,' he said, and I was pushed off the plane and interviewed by a poker-faced customs officer, who stamped my passport before I was taken to the baggage carousel.

Now I've travelled through miles of corridor to reach two white doors that are gliding open automatically in front of me. As I'm pushed through them, I see a long metal barrier with people standing on the other side of it. Some are holding up signs that they wave in my direction; others are gathered in small family groups with expectant faces. Dozens of eyes flick over me before people realise I'm not who they were hoping to see. Signs droop and faces look away as they prepare to carry on their wait. I look around, scanning faces and feeling nervous that there has been a mistake and Joanna won't be here to greet me. What would I do then?

'Martin?'

I turn my head. She's here. I can hardly breathe. She is more beautiful than I ever thought possible. She smiles at me as she leans down.

'My liefie,' she says in Afrikaans. 'My love.'

I feel awkward for a moment before our arms close around each other. Then, as I hold her for the first time, I realise that she smells of sweets and flowers. I know that I will never let go of her again.

I am home.

54

Together

I am drunk, intoxicated by everything that is happening to me for the first time: seeing her smile when she looks up at me sitting opposite her and losing myself in her kiss, watching her eyebrows knit together as she tries to decide what she wants to eat from a restaurant menu or sitting together underneath a hornbeam tree in the pouring rain.

'My liefie,' she says over and over, as if trying to convince herself that I'm really here. 'My love.'

We've come to Scotland after spending a few days at Joanna's flat, where we celebrated her birthday with Kim and some friends. But now we are all alone and we've hardly seen the rolling hills and sky that lowers and glimmers by turns outside our cottage. Instead we stay indoors, sitting or lying side by side, always connected by a hand within a hand, a shoulder against a shoulder or a leg carelessly thrown across a lap. After all these months of longing for each other, we can't bear to be apart even for a moment.

I've hardly used the alphabet board. Instead I draw letters on her skin with my finger, words traced on her flesh that she can read. In many ways they are almost useless. We've said enough after so many months of talking and often don't need words because Joanna understands so much just by looking at my face. An eyebrow or a glance is usually enough to answer many of her practical questions. Whatever fleeting thoughts I'd had before I arrived about whether we'd stutter politely as we wondered what to say or self-consciously try to entertain each other with jokes have come to nothing. From the moment we met at the airport, we have drunk each other in, comfortable in one other's presence.

I've never known a person who accepts me so completely and has so much peace inside them. Joanna doesn't fill the spaces between us with mindless chatter. Instead we drift on the current of simply being together and there are times when I jump almost in surprise as she touches me – my fingers flexing when she strokes my hand or my jaw twitching when she kisses my eyes. It's as if my body can't quite believe her gentleness. I've never had someone take pleasure in me before. It is the simplest but most perfect of feelings.

We are cartographers of each other's skin, following the lines of each other's cheeks, jaws and hands with our fingertips, imprinting the feel of each other onto ourselves for hour after hour. Her hands fit perfectly into mine and I stroke the scar she got when she caught her hand in the chicken coop as a child. I didn't realise that love would pierce all of my senses as it has: every part of me is attuned to her as I watch her smile, breathe in her smell, listen to her voice, taste her kisses and touch her skin.

The one thing we don't do is make love to each other. We agreed before I arrived that we would wait because we have the rest of our lives, after all. I haven't proposed but Joanna and I know we will marry. We discussed it even before I got here and know that I'm going to move to the UK in order for us to start a life together here. It amazes me how easily we can make such decisions; it's as if we are each an extension of the other. I revel in such simplicity after a life in which even the most inconsequential things can be complicated. Making love to each other will be the final piece of our jigsaw together. We will save it for our wedding night.

For now it feels as if Joanna is healing all that has been dammed inside me for so long as we learn more about each other day by day. I'm used to people trying to cajole me into doing things or wanting me to sit passively while they do everything for me. But Joanna accepts me as I am today and doesn't mourn what I once was. What surprises me most, though, is that she seems almost uninterested in my rehabilitation. She doesn't push me to do things or raise an eyelid if I can't. It doesn't matter to her that I only have my alphabet board here because it wasn't practical to bring my old laptop with me. She doesn't want to hear my 'voice'. Nor does she hover like a mother waiting to pick up a crawling child. Instead she helps me only as and when I need it. She trusts me to know my own body while accepting that there are some days when it can do less than it can on others.

'It's not you that's not working, it's your hands,' she told me one day when I got frustrated while struggling to pull on a jumper. 'Just give them a rest and try again tomorrow.'

Even the unwitting mistakes she sometimes makes don't panic or embarrass her as they would so many others.

'My liefie!' she cried as she came in one morning to find me sprawled across the bed.

She'd left me getting dressed but I'd lost my balance as I pulled on my jumper and toppled over like a fallen oak.

'Are you okay?' Joanna said with a giggle as she helped me up. 'I must make sure I prop you up better next time!'

She didn't apologise in embarrassed confusion or feel guilty that she'd done something wrong, and her simplicity made me feel at ease. Instead she just smiled before kissing me and leaving the room so I could finish dressing. If she does want to say something, then she does it matter-of-factly, as she did a few mornings ago when I bent down to drain my coffee cup as I always do.

'I don't understand why you always drink and eat so quickly,' Joanna said. 'It's like you're always in a rush.'

For a moment, I hardly knew what she meant. I've never eaten or drunk slowly. These have always been hurried activities, mere refuelling exercises to be got out of the way as soon as possible because people spend precious time helping me to do them. I've hardly even considered savouring food or drink. But that evening Joanna gave me my first-ever spoon of crème caramel and I made myself slow down long enough to taste it. First there was sweetness, then the dark richness of caramel as it flooded over my tongue, followed by the faintest hint of bitterness and finally the richness of cream with the scent of vanilla above it.

'You look so happy,' Joanna said.

She has told me that the pleasure I take in things is one of the greatest joys I give her. She says that she has never seen anyone revel in things as much as I do and it makes her happy to see that the world astounds me so often because there are almost as many new things as there are ways to experience joy.

But until now these have been mostly private thoughts and it is a pleasure to share my joy so completely with Joanna. She laughs when my eyes open wide at a crimson sunset or I smile in wonder as we drive around a bend in the road to see the beauty of an emerald green landscape stretching out ahead of us.

Her acceptance of me is the reason I've started trying to do more since I got here. She makes me want to start trusting a body that I lost confidence in so long ago. A couple of mornings ago, after a week of watching Joanna in the kitchen, I decided it was my turn to try. I'd never made so much as a cup of coffee on my own before because my shaking hands are a liability that few people will trust in a kitchen. But Joanna had cooked for me all week and didn't say a word when I told her it was my turn to make breakfast.

After fastening a foam grip on my right hand to help me pick up small objects like knives and spoons, she loosened the tops of the coffee and jam jars that she knew I would never be able to open on my own before turning to leave.

'I'm going to read my book,' she said.

I stared at the kettle in front of me. I wouldn't dare to try to pour boiling water but I could flick the switch to heat it. I turned the kettle on before looking at the jar of coffee on the counter in front of me. It was almost at eye level and I fixed it in my sights as I stretched my hand out and leaned as far forward in my chair as I possibly could. My fingers closed around the jar as I pulled it towards me and knocked off the lid. Then I picked up a spoon, my very particular kind of nemesis – a tiny object that my unfeeling hands won't close around properly.

The spoon clattered in my shaking hand as I pushed it inside the jar and dug into the coffee. Grains flew off the trembling spoon as I tried pulling it out and the last remaining few scattered across the counter when I finally did. Frustration burned. I wished I could command my unruly hands to submit to my will just once. Once, twice, three times I tried to get a spoonful of coffee into two cups before moving on to the sugar. By the time I knew I was beaten, one cup contained enough coffee to make syrupy tar and the other a watery imitation. It was a start.

Next came the toast. Joanna had left some slices of bread in the toaster and I pushed the switch down before pulling myself along the worktop to reach the butter and jam. I put them on my lap before pushing myself off from the counter towards the table, where I left them. Then I pushed off across the kitchen once again to get to the cupboard where the plates were kept. Bending down, I opened it and took out what I needed before going back to the table and laying it.

Finally I needed knives. Whoever said that breakfast is the simplest meal of the day? It didn't seem like it to me. There were so many different things to get right. The toast had popped up and was getting cold, and the water in the kettle had boiled. I needed to hurry if I wanted Joanna to have something warm.

I got two knives out of a drawer, dropped the toast into my lap and pushed off for a final time towards the table. Although

I wasn't going to fill up the coffee cups, I was determined to try spreading the toast at least. I put it and one of the knives on the table before picking up the other and trying to steady it as it waved about wildly in the air. Pushing the blade towards the butter, I watched as it crashed through the top and out again. I stared at the huge crevasse I'd carved in what had been a perfect rectangular pat of yellow before jerking the knife down towards the toast. A yellow slick of butter appeared halfway across it.

Now for the jam — my final Everest. I pulled the jar towards me and thrust my knife into it. It clattered inside the jar before skidding off in the opposite direction to the toast when I pulled it out. I forced the knife downwards, cleaving it to my will as it hit the side of the toast before skittering across the plate and leaving a glistening red slick on the table. I stared at the battered toast before looking at the floor, which was covered in coffee granules and sugar. The butter looked as if a wild animal had chewed it and jam had erupted like a volcano across the table.

Euphoria filled me. I'd made toast, coffee was waiting in the cups and the water had boiled   Joanna was going to have breakfast. I banged a spoon on the table to let her know I was ready and a smile spread across her face as she walked in.

'How nice to have breakfast made for me!' she said.

As she sat down, I vowed that I would learn to do more for her, teach my body to listen to my commands more closely so that I could look after her better in the future.

'My liefie,' Joanna said as she studied the table before looking at me. 'You don't have to use a knife, you know.'

I raised my eyebrows in disbelief.

'Why not just use your hand next time?' she said. 'It would be far easier for you that way. It doesn't matter how you do something, does it, as long as you find a way?'

Without another word, we ate our toast together. Later I raised my hand to stroke her cheek. At last I understood what love was. I knew I'd never feel about another woman the way I did about Joanna. She was everything I would ever need.

55

I Can't Choose

'Martin?'

I hold on to the box I'm carrying like a shield I'm trusting to protect me from attack.

'Martin? Are you okay?'

I can't look at her. I'm frozen. Lights glare above me and music pumps out from stereo speakers. Teenagers shriek as they walk around my chair and a wall of trainers rises up in front of me. I'm supposed to pick one from pair after pair stacked one above the other but I can't do it. I don't know how.

'Do you want white or a colour?'

'Nike or Adidas?'

'Classics, hi-tops or skate shoes?'

'Below £50 or above £100?'

At first, I enjoyed the fact that shop assistants spoke to me here in England. But now all I can think about is the pair of brown leather shoes in the box on my lap that Joanna has just bought for me. She has already spent so much money; I don't deserve more.

'Would you like to try something on?' the assistant asks. 'Or shall I measure your feet?'

I stare at my black, sturdy shoes. I've had them for about eight years and they are built up at the ankles to support my feet. I'd never thought about owning another pair. These are my shoes. I wear them every day. When I'm not wearing them, I have slippers. But when Joanna suggested that I might want something new, I agreed because I didn't know what else to say. But what will I do with three pairs of shoes?

I know that I must make a decision and show that I know my own mind. If not, Joanna will see the truth that I've been trying to hide from her for so long. It's a secret I've kept for all the months that we've known each other. I've hidden it so well that I've prevented it from being brought out into the open. But now there is nothing else I can do to conceal it: I'm not worthy of her. How will I ever be a good husband if I can't even pick a pair of shoes? I'm lost in Joanna's world, where there are constant decisions to be made – what to eat, where to go and when to do things. As soon as one decision is made, it feels as if another is snapping at its heels and I feel overwhelmed by choices I'm not used to making.

'What cereal would you like?' Joanna asked me on our first trip to the supermarket.

I gazed at the tapestry of primary-coloured cardboard boxes on the shelves in front of me and realised I had no idea how to start making a decision. How did people ever get anything done with their days when just choosing what to eat at the start of them could take hours? It was the same with everything in the supermarket: there wasn't one kind of soup but thirty, not one loaf of bread but a hundred.

Seeing that I couldn't decide, Joanna asked me to tell her what I wanted to eat but I couldn't even do that. I forgot long ago what it was to be hungry or to yearn for a particular food after teaching myself to ignore the sensation of a gnawing stomach or a craving I knew I could never satisfy. Now I can occasionally decide on something I want to eat but I can't choose enough to fill a whole shopping trolley the way other people do.

I stare up at the trainers again. I've been waiting for this moment to come. I knew I would be forced to make a decision for myself sometime, but Joanna refused to listen. Instead she tried to reassure me that I could cope in her world so I've tried to make her see the error of her ways by asking her again and again exactly why she loves me.

'Because you are a good, kind man who is unlike anyone I've ever known,' she says. 'Because you're intelligent and thoughtful, warm and wise. Because you love so completely and have taught me to slow down and take notice of a world that I've spent so long rushing past.

'There are so many reasons, Martin: your smile, the way you look at me. I can't tell you them all.'

Her reassurances mean little now though. I can't even decide what shoes I want. She's going to realise that deep down I still don't understand adult life. My fear of the world feels like a boulder that weighs heavy inside me, a shadow that is threatening to blot out all of her light. I'm not what she thinks I am. I'm a fraud.

'What a beautiful man,' she said a few days ago when she was shaving me.

As Joanna smiled at me in the mirror, I couldn't smile back. In fact, I felt almost frozen because I'd never heard a woman call me a man before. I'd longed to hear those words from a woman for so long but I also felt afraid when I did because it had taken me years to accept that I was an adult. When Joanna looked at me in the mirror, I couldn't bring myself to stare back at my own reflection because I couldn't believe what she was saying.

'Look at yourself, Martin,' she told me gently. 'Please just look at yourself.'

She wouldn't have told me I was a man if she knew the truth: that when we met Kim and Joanna's friends to celebrate her birthday, I felt overwhelmed being among so many people I didn't know; that when I look at restaurant menus, I don't know what many of the foods are, let alone if I want to eat them; that apologies for something I'm sure I've done wrong bubble up inside me almost every minute.

It's not that I don't want to be what Joanna thinks I am. All I want is to protect her and keep her safe. But as she looks at me now, I realise it doesn't matter what I want; I'm not the kind of man Joanna needs. She will never be able to depend on me. I'm so overwhelmed by the world now that I'm trying to step out of the tiny strip of it I've come to know and understand.

'Martin, my love,' Joanna says. 'Are you okay?'

My heart thuds in panic as I raise my head. Her face

shimmers in front of me as my eyes fill with tears. There is nothing I can do to stop them as they start to fall. Sitting in the middle of the shop, I begin to weep as I feel her arms close around me.

56

Fred and Ginger

There are so many moments with her that I will never forget and this is one of them. It is about 11 p.m. and we are in Trafalgar Square in central London. After spending the day visiting sights and going to the theatre, we are now in the middle of this vast square. Above us, Nelson stands on his column keeping watch over London. He is guarded by four huge lions and there is a fountain illuminated by lights. It is dark at last. The light doesn't fade in England until late in the evening but now the sky above us is black. Soon we must leave but first there is something we must do.

My head is full of pictures from the last two weeks, snapshots that I will take back with me when I leave: lifting Joanna in my arms for the first time when we went swimming and the water supported me enough to hold her; entering York Minster and feeling overwhelmed by the beauty of the cathedral — the stone and light, peace and tranquillity — as I felt her hand in mine; sitting in a rose garden together and eating lunch in the sun; inhaling the smell of fresh coffee as she sat opposite me and I realised with wonder that we were together at last. There were so many memories to keep safe: falling asleep beside her even as characters roared on the cinema screen in front of us, smiling at her face as she tried to swallow bitter Scottish whisky and watching her smile at me as we sat together in Sherwood Forest.

Now we are silent as we look at each other. There were so many things that we dreamed of doing before we met and this is one of them. I take her hand as I push against the concrete with my feet. I move gently forwards in my chair as I guide Joanna around me in a circle. I look at her and know she can hear the music that I hear too. It is a happy tune – not too fast, not too slow. She laughs as she spins around and her hair is lifted a little by the breeze. Joy rushes through me. We are dancing.

Joanna (Joan) and Martin – June 2008

57

Leaving

If I ever felt that Joanna was a dream, then this is the moment I know for sure she's real. Pain pierces me as I watch her cry. I'm leaving the UK today and it will be two months before we meet again in Canada. As I look at her, I tell myself that we must look forward to the end of the year, when she will fly to South Africa for Christmas before we return to England to start a life together. That is what we've decided we're going to do but for now we won't tell anyone until we've made our final plans. It all feels so far away though, as I kiss Joanna's cheek. She's quiet as she sits up and wipes away her tears.

'What will I do without you, my liefie?' she asks as she leans forward to kiss me.

I look at her and know she understands all that I want to say. She pulls away and stands up with a sigh.

'I'll put the bags in the car,' she says. 'We'll need to leave soon.'

Her fingers trail slowly out of my hand, as if she wants to

stay connected to me for as long as she can. But we both know that we must give in to the inevitable as she leaves the room. My heart feels like a stone in my chest as I look at the open doorway but I must be strong for Joanna after all the reassurance she has given me.

'I understand things won't always be this way,' she told me after I explained my fears that she'd unwisely chosen a man so disoriented by her world. 'This was just the first visit and you were bound to feel overwhelmed. I know it won't last forever because you'll get used to life here.

'I know what a strong, capable man you are, Martin. Look at all you've achieved. Please don't let this trip make you doubt yourself.'

As she smiled at me, I knew I would never tire of sitting at a table and talking with her. It's one of the greatest pleasures we share and we are often the last to leave restaurants.

'Good on you, son,' an old man said to me one day as he walked past our table and saw Joanna and I talking.

We both looked at him, unsure what he meant.

'For learning your alphabet!' he said, as he pointed to my board.

But our laughter seems so far away now as I turn my head to look around the empty room. I can already feel the pain of missing Joanna. I try to push it down. I mustn't give in to it. I have to be strong for her. But the pain keeps rising higher. Everything has changed in just two weeks. I've got used to seeing her first thing in the morning and last thing at night, and feeling her touch again and again during the day. Now I must go back to my old life. But how can I when I'd waited so long to find her?

My chest tightens and the pain sharpens. I gulp in air as I hear a muffled half noise, a rasping gasp of pain. It comes from nowhere. I look around. The room is empty. I made the noise. It is the first sound I've ever heard myself make. It is the low yelp of a wounded animal.

58

A Fork in the Road

This conversation has been hanging in the air like a bird waiting to swoop ever since I got home.

'You disappeared,' my father says as he sits down opposite me. 'You should have let us know where you were and what you were doing. Your mother was frantic when we didn't hear from you.'

I don't think his heart is really in this conversation but I've been expecting it ever since Kim took me to one side just before I left the UK.

'Mum and Dad have been really worried,' she said. 'And Dad was very upset that you didn't get in touch on Father's Day.'

I wasn't sure this was completely true. Both my parents are used to knowing everything I do, when and how, but I think my mother would have struggled most when I forgot my family for the first time. My head is so full of the future, though, that I can hardly think about the present as my father chastises me.

Joanna and I have only the Internet and the phone once again and I wonder how we ever survived for the first six months of knowing each other. It is far harder to be apart from her now than it was before we met.

But instead of driving myself mad by counting down every hour of each day until I get on the plane to Canada, I'm trying to keep myself busy with other things. My biggest distraction at the moment is a ring I'm having made for Joanna. It's a copy of one she bought cheaply but loves and I've asked a jeweller to make it using real gold overlaid with a pattern of intertwined leaves encrusted with tiny emeralds. I'm going to give it to Joanna on the day that I ask her to be my wife.

'Martin?'

My father looks at me.

'Are you listening?'

Sometimes I'm glad that I don't have to say anything.

'Well, then do you agree that you have a responsibility to let people know how you are?' he asks me. 'I know you were busy with more important things when you were away but you should have kept in touch.'

I nod.

My father's face relaxes a little as he stands up to leave. For the moment he is reassured. His world is back in place because I'm home again. As he walks out of the room, I realise for the first time how hard it will be for my parents when I tell them that I'm moving to the UK to be with Joanna. I'm not just leaving home, I'm moving across the world. While teenagers might fight thoughtlessly against their parents when they are trying to break free, it is impossible for me not to know that altering the course of my life will change my parents' lives forever too.

59

Confessions

I didn't realise that dreams are in constant motion until I
looked back at mine and saw how much they'd changed.
I made this discovery when Joanna and I were in Canada. At
the conference we attended Diane Bryen's dream workshop,
as I'd done several times since that first one at the communication centre.

'What would you like me to draw?' Joanna asked as we sat
together.

I remembered all the times I'd asked myself what I
dared to dream since meeting Diane. All I wanted when I
first asked myself the question was to be able to communicate more and go out into the world. Once I'd achieved that
and started working, I dreamed of living a more independent life and finding someone to share it with. Now I've met
Joanna and her dream is mine too – a wedding and a house
together.

These things are almost within our reach now because ever

since I returned from the UK, I've been applying for a visa to move to England. My parents know I'm going through the process, just as my brother David is, but we haven't spoken about it in any detail because I've been reluctant to discuss my plans until they are fully in place. But I knew as I sat in the dream workshop that I had to start trying to tell people what I wanted from my life, so I told them that Joanna and I were planning to marry.

Word soon spread because I'm well known in the AAC community to academics and experts, fellow users and their families. Although I'd feared some people might resent me for leaving my life in South Africa and all the work I've done here, my friends and colleagues were more positive than I'd dared hope. All of them celebrated with us and I've been counting down the weeks until I leave for England ever since.

Leaving my parents will be hard, of course, and knowing that I must soon part from Kojak is almost impossible – we've been constant companions. Although Joanna has looked into the possibility of taking him to England, we both know it wouldn't work because he wouldn't be able to bear spending six months in quarantine. I'm sure that Mum and Dad will agree to keep him because they're almost fond of him now, but even so I dread the moment when it comes to saying goodbye.

I've put off telling my parents about our plans because I want them to be concrete first. Now they are. In just a few weeks, Joanna arrives in South Africa for Christmas, after which I will fly back to the UK with her. That's why I can't put off the inevitable any longer and tonight I want to tell my parents that I'm planning to propose to Joanna while she's here.

'I'd like to speak to you,' I tell them as the three of us sit working at our desks in the study.

As they look at me, I think of all the hours we've spent together in this room. First we researched communication devices and then tested them out. Next the study was filled with cardboard boxes full of equipment and I watched as my parents patiently loaded software onto my computer. I remember the wonder I felt as I realised that soon I would have so many words to say, all the months my mother sat with me for hour after hour, week after week, helping me to learn to communicate and the excitement that energised Mum and Dad on the day they watched me slowly clicking on enough symbols to say a sentence for the first time.

They were equally proud when I was offered a job at the health centre and when they found out that I'd been accepted on a university course. They've been with me for every step of my journey into the wider world: accompanying me to conferences and meetings; filling out forms and helping me to travel; sitting through lectures and standing by my side as I've been introduced to people; encouraging and cajoling me when I'm down and celebrating my successes. They've also looked after every one of my daily practical needs whether we were at home or away. Instead of slipping into comfortable middle age, they've devoted themselves to looking after me and all I can hope now is that they understand why I'm leaving.

Since returning from my trip to England, I've seen their initial worries about Joanna slowly fade. They understand now that our relationship is real and they're pleased that I have someone in my life to care about. My mother has told me that she's never seen me so happy. My parents ask about Joanna, chat with her over the Internet sometimes and are looking forward to having her here with us for Christmas. Now I hope they'll be happy to welcome her into our family permanently and understand why I must leave them to make a new life.

'What is it?' Mum asks as she and Dad sit down beside me. 'Has something happened?'

I've prepared something to say and they watch as I press a button and bring up the message on the screen.

'There's something I want to tell you and I hope you will be happy,' they read.

Neither of them says a word as they read what I want to tell them.

'As you know, Joanna and I are very much in love but there is something else you need to know.

'When she arrives here in December, I'm going to ask Joanna to marry me and after Christmas we are planning to go back to the UK together.

'We have been talking about it for months and I know this is the right thing for me to do. I hope you will be happy for me.'

I put my hand into my pocket and pull out the ring I've had made for Joanna. My parents stare at it and neither of them speaks for a moment.

'It's beautiful,' Mum says eventually. 'Oh, Martin! It's beautiful.'

She starts to laugh and my father does too. Relief floods over me.

'Congratulations, boy!' Dad says as he puts his arm around me. 'It's wonderful news.'

He leans towards me.

'We're so proud of you,' he says.

My parents are happy. They understand the time has come to let me go.

60

Up, Up and Away

It's dark outside as I wait for Joanna to get dressed but it will soon be sunrise. I've told her we are doing something special but she doesn't know what it is. All I've said is that she must wear light cotton clothes because it'll soon be hot. It's December and the days can be scorching. Joanna has just arrived for Christmas and we're spending a couple of nights together at a farm in the bush. It's been four months since we last saw each other and I know she's as thankful as I am that we'll never have to say goodbye again. On Boxing Day — six days short of a year since we were first introduced — we'll fly back to the UK to start our new life.

The ring I've had made for Joanna is hidden in my pocket, secured to my waistband by cotton thread so that it will be safe even if my shaking hands drop it when I ask her to marry me. I can hardly believe I'm sitting here about to propose to her. Is it possible? Could my life really have changed so much or is this a dream like the ones I used to lose myself in for weeks at a time when I was a ghost boy? I dare not pinch myself because I might wake up and I never want that to happen.

Joanna arrived three days ago and, after meeting my parents, she took me to see her mother on the farm where she lives. I'd been writing to Joanna's mother for several months, knowing that I would one day ask her for her daughter's hand and now I handed her a final letter.

'I would like to ask Joanna to marry me,' it said. 'But first I would like to ask you for your blessing.'

For the longest moment, her mother said nothing before she smiled at me. She is a generous woman who can recognise love when she sees it – even if it comes in a form that some people can't appreciate.

I look up and smile as Joanna walks into the room.

'I'm ready,' she says as she walks towards me.

She is silhouetted against a white wall in the half-light. My heart skips a beat. She is so beautiful.

We go outside into the cool morning air and get into the car we've hired. I tell Joanna which way to go, but as we drive further into the bush, she doesn't ask where we are going any more. Does she know what I'm planning or does she think this is just another of the everyday surprises that I often give her?

As we drive up a dusty dirt road towards a clearing in the savannah, I see the carcass of a hot air balloon lying on the ground ahead of us. Joanna has always wanted to see the earth from the sky and she laughs as she realises what is waiting for her.

'I can't believe you've done this!' she says as she turns and kisses me.

The two of us get out of the car. The balloonist in charge

of our trip is waiting in the grey morning light and soon the orange fires of the balloon's burner start to illuminate the darkness as slivers of light appear on the horizon. The sun is rising and soon we'll see it from the clouds. Joanna and I watch as the balloon slowly ascends from where it has been lying before getting into the basket when it's ready. I sit on a high stool so that I'm level with Joanna and hold on to the edge of the basket as she climbs in after me.

The balloon pilot smiles to let us know that we are about to take off and the basket lifts silently off the ground. I watch Joanna's face as we begin to float upwards. She is smiling as she stares at the bush disappearing below us. We rise up higher and I look out at the horizon. It's getting lighter now. The sky is pink and the muted colours of the bush below us are slowly being illuminated green and brown. The earth rushes away as I listen to the silence. It's so quiet up here that all we can hear is the rush of the balloon's burner and the occasional birdcall.

Joanna and I put our arms around each other as the sun rises higher in the sky – bright white behind grey clouds, then pink lightening the darkness with flashes of orange. The horizon that was black in front of us is gradually turning golden in the sun and we can see the earth beneath us: a river, trees and a waterfall falling into a valley; zebra galloping, wildebeest and warthog drinking at a waterhole, giraffe feeding from tree branches.

'It's so beautiful,' Joanna tells me.

It's time now. I put my hand into my pocket and pull out my mobile phone. I've recorded a message on it, words that I want Joanna to hear. She looks at me as I hand her some tiny earphones and she puts them into her ears before I press a button.

'There are no words in any language that will ever truly capture what I feel for you,' I tell her. 'You came into my life and gave meaning to it. You flooded my otherwise grey world with vivid colour and I feel like I've known you forever.

'It's like time stops when we are together. You give my heart not just a reason to beat but to sing and rejoice.'

She smiles as she looks at me and I squeeze her hand.

'With every passing day my love for you gets stronger and deeper, richer and more profound because you are beautiful inside and out,' I say. 'And while life is not all milk and roses – and sometimes we eat a little salt too – what I do know is that I don't work without you and I don't want to spend a moment of my life without you.

'You are my soulmate, my best friend, my companion, my lover, my rock and strength, my soft place to fall in this crazy world.

'And that is why I want to hold you, cherish you, take care of you, protect you and love you with everything I have.

'So will you do me the honour, the enormous privilege, of sharing the rest of my life with me and becoming my wife?'

I push my hand into my pocket and pull out the ring. There are tears in Joanna's eyes as I hold it up to her – a pool of gold hanging by a thread that glints in the early morning light. She bends towards me.

'Yes, my liefie,' she says. 'I will be proud to be your wife.'

She kisses me for the longest moment before pulling away. I wrap my arms around her as we look out to the horizon. It stretches out endlessly in front of us.

Newly engaged couple

61

Saying Goodbye

The cardboard box sits on the other side of the room but I'm not sure I want to see what's inside it. The box is full of the Lego that I have been told I loved so much as a child. But do I have the strength to invoke the phantom of the ghost boy again and see his withered limbs and empty eyes rise up in front of me? I've seen him so many times over recent days, I'm not sure I can confront him again.

Joanna and I are packing up as I prepare to leave for England. As well as everyday belongings, we've been sorting through the boxes my parents have kept over the years and I've learned that much of what happened to me has been captured in dispiriting mementoes of my past: old X-rays and medical records packed side by side with the hand splints that once kept my fingers from curling into claws; an old cushion for my wheelchair stacked on top of the bibs that once caught my drool. While for me each object makes a memory resurface, it's vividly brought my story to life for Joanna for the first time.

She's only known me since I've grown so much stronger but now she can see all that I once was and the extent of my parents' vain hopes captured forever in spoons with oversized handles that they once thought I would learn to grip again.

At times I've felt shocked by what I've seen because as I rushed forward into life I'd almost forgotten how sick I was. Although I've sensed how hard it's been for Joanna, I also know there is no one else on earth I could have done this with. I would have felt ashamed for anyone else to see this and uncomfortable to have had so many bad memories dragged up again in front of them. But with Joanna here, the only feeling that's filled me as I've watched the ghost boy come back to life is sadness that his existence was so wretched.

Yesterday my mother told me there was another stash of boxes in the garage but both she and my father seemed reluctant to get them for me. I realised why when Joanna and I found them. While Kim and David's boxes were stuffed with the belongings of a teenager's life – music tapes and study files, old posters and clothes – mine, piled in a corner of the garage, yellowed with age and covered with dust, contained only a child's toys. It was as if a boy had died and his life had been hurriedly packed away – then I remembered he had.

'Look at this!' Joanna said, after dragging some of the boxes inside and opening one.

In her hand was a multicoloured cuddly toy.

'His name was Popple,' my mother said quietly.

I looked up to see her standing in the doorway, as if afraid to step into the room and see the rest of what we were unpacking.

'He was Martin's favourite,' she said.

I looked at the toy, trying to remember a time when an orange cuddly dog with lime-green hair, red ears, a purple nose and blue paws was my favourite thing in the world. I wanted to remember so much. I long to have the kind of memories other people do and know what it feels like to be a child who loves a toy so much that he can't let it go. But however hard I've searched, I've never been able to find even a glimmer of a memory inside me. There is nothing there – not even a shred of an image that I can cling on to.

But it was comforting for me to see a link to a past I'd sometimes wondered existed at all, even though I knew that it was a painful reminder of all they'd lost for my parents. As Mum stood by me while Joanna unpacked more boxes – a wooden horse GD had made for me, the telegram announcing my birth and schoolbooks – I could feel her distress. Mum said nothing when Joanna found a single piece of ruled notepaper in the bottom of one box. On it was written a letter I'd sent to Father Christmas when I was eight years old, the words almost painfully neat on the page. I read it slowly, trying to hear myself in the words I'd written so long before.

Dear Father Christmas,
Thank you for our presents last year. They were just the presents I wanted. Here are some of the things I would like for this Christmas: a speedometer, a skateboard, Meccano, space Lego, water bottle for my bike, a solar cell, a radio-controlled car.
Father Christmas, I'll ask my father to leave the Christmas tree lights on. Father Christmas, in my list I

mention Meccano. If you decide to give me Meccano
could you give me electronic Meccano?
    Your loyal present receiver,
    Martin Pistorius

PS I will leave a glass with some things to drink in it if
I can and some things to eat. I will ask my father if we
can leave the Christmas tree lights on. We will leave our
stockings where the tree is.
PPS Also a walkie-talkie set.

I felt both sadness and joy when I looked at that letter – sadness that I couldn't remember being that happy little boy and joy that I was once him. Then I looked at my mother and saw that her face had frozen as she'd listened to his words. None of us spoke as Joanna put the note carefully back into the box and closed the lid.

'Shall we stop for today?' she said.

Now we are back in the room with the boxes once again and I'm looking at the one that contains my Lego. When Joanna opens it, I see a mass of pieces: some tiny, some large, some broken and others covered in dirt. There are so many of them that the box is almost full to the brim and I know there are at least another two like this.

'It was always your favourite,' Mum says. 'You so loved playing with it. You would spend hours in here building it. That Lego was your favourite thing in the world. You were such a bright little boy.'

Her voice is full of sadness. Tears are barely contained within it.

'I should never have let David have it,' she says. 'He asked me again and again and I always said no until one day I finally agreed. He was never as careful as you with his toys.'

As she stares at the box, I know she is seeing a happy, healthy little boy who once smiled in delight as he pieced together brightly coloured plastic blocks.

'I gave it to your brother because I thought you weren't going to want it again,' Mum says quietly. 'I didn't think you would ever come back to me.'

As my mother looks at me and admits that she stopped believing in hope, I know the wounds of the past are in some ways still as fresh for her today as they ever were. While the child who loved Lego is just a stranger to me, he is all too real for my parents. He is the child they loved and lost.

62

Letting Go

I'm sitting on a bed at the farm where Joanna's mother lives. In a few days we will return to England. Joanna has just packed up the last of my Lego after washing it. Although I'll be taking it to the UK with me, I don't feel content that my past has been neatly sorted through and repacked. Instead I've felt a sadness lying in the pit of my stomach ever since I left my parents' house, and it's getting heavier and heavier as the days pass.

I keep remembering my mother's face as she looked at my Lego. She seemed so lost, so wounded, and I'm sure my father is suffering as well even though he hides his feelings better. I can't stop thinking about them, about me and the happy child I found hidden in those boxes. I'd never truly understood what he was like until I opened them up and found a boy who loved electronics and Meccano, who wrote politely to Father Christmas and adored his parents. I can't stop thinking of him now.

My tears come slowly at first, running silently down my cheeks as Joanna looks up.

'Martin?' she exclaims.

She gets up from the floor and puts her arms around me. My breath comes in heavy gasps and my shoulders heave as I think about all that my parents, brother, sister and I have lost. Guilt fills me as I think about the pain I've caused and wish I could take it back. If only I could give my family the simple, happy life they deserved. Then confusion swells up as I wonder why my parents took so long to rescue me. Why didn't they see that I'd come back to them and protect me from harm? Finally I cry for all the love they gave to a child who slowly sickened, for the devotion they've shown me ever since and for the little boy I've only just met but will never truly know however much I might wish to. All I have of him are scraps of paper and old toys and I know he will never seem real to me. He'll be a sprite, a memory captured in fading photographs of someone I'll never know.

Joanna hugs me even tighter as tears flood out of me. I cry and cry, unable to stop myself from grieving for all that has been lost for so many people. But as she holds me, I know that Joanna will never have to comfort me like this again. A dam has been broken inside as I've confronted the past. Now I'm mourning it. One day soon I hope to say a final goodbye.

63

A New Life

Our flat in the UK is so small that my electric wheelchair is too big to fit into it, I can only move freely up and down one small strip of corridor in my manual chair and I've burned myself repeatedly trying to master the kettle and the toaster. I've set a dishcloth on fire and used furniture polish to clean the kitchen tiles. But for me the two-metre sweep of floor that I can negotiate is my very own Hollywood Boulevard, the garden I see outside the window is the Alhambra and the tiny kitchen where I try to cook is the finest Parisian restaurant. I was wrong to think for so long that the only worthwhile challenges were to be found at work or in my studies when there are so many in everyday life.

I've become stronger in the months since arriving in England and I can now move around quite easily in the small part of the flat that is accessible to my chair by pushing off the floorboards with my feet. My arms aren't yet strong enough to control my chair but I can sit up well all day now. My left hand is still unreliable but my right is getting steadier all the time. I hardly ever try to use both. Instead I do everything with my right arm and my body seems to like being pushed in new directions because my failures are matched by successes: I'm not so good at opening bottles but I can now get coffee into cups; I can't yet tie my shoelaces but I'm able to push the vacuum cleaner around the wooden floor.

So much of everyday life, though, is literally above me. I feel useless as I watch Joanna hanging curtains or I stare at things in cupboards soaring overhead. After deciding to cook supper one night, I tried to dislodge a bag of flour from a shelf using a broom and watched it hurtle down towards me, knowing there was nothing I could do to stop it. Joanna found me – and the rest of the flat – covered in flour when she got home that night.

My worst mistake came when I tried to garden. Joanna had looked for a flat with a garden for so long that I was anxious to keep it perfect. So when dandelions started bursting bright yellow through the grass, I decided that something had to be done. But after I'd carefully sprayed the dandelions – and the rest of the lawn – with weedkiller, we woke up the next day to find that the grass had turned yellow. All we could do was watch its final death throes as we realised what I'd done wrong. Joanna and I have scattered the ground with seeds now and we hope that the rain that falls so steadily in England will encourage a new lawn to grow.

I'm working freelance as a web designer but the rest of my time is devoted to being a house husband in training. I enjoy learning how to look after a home and Joanna chastises me so little for my mistakes that I wonder if she realises quite how inept I am.

'What shall we do?' she wailed when we found a nail sticking out of one of our car tyres.

I had no idea.

'Shall I pull it out?' Joanna asked me.

It is becoming more and more clear to me that she assumes there is a long list of internal practical data hidden inside me simply because I'm a man. But after realising that I had no advice to give, Joanna bent down and pulled the nail out. As air hissed out of the tyre and we watched it slowly flatten, we looked at each other and laughed.

'We'll know what not to do next time,' she said.

But there have also been times when her patience has worn a little thinner and recently she turned to me as we were getting ready to go out one weekend morning.

'Shall we go to the supermarket first or the chemist?' she asked.

I wasn't sure. I still find planning my days so hard that I'm happy to follow the pattern Joanna wants them to follow.

'I don't mind,' I typed.

But instead of getting up from her chair and chattering to me as she usually does, Joanna didn't move.

'What's wrong?' I typed on the small portable keyboard she's given me to use instead of my alphabet board.

'Nothing,' she said.

But still she didn't move.

'Are you sure?'

'Completely.'

We sit together silently.

'I'm just waiting,' Joanna said eventually.

'For what?'

'For you to decide what we're going to do this morning. I'm tired and I want you to make a decision.

'I know you can do it because I've seen you at work. You were the centre of attention at the conference in Canada and you're completely in control in that world – you guide people and reassure them, advise and lead them.

'So now I want you to do the same at home. I know you're not used to it but I'm tired of making all the decisions, my liefie. So that's why I'm going to sit here until you decide what you want us to do today.'

I wasn't sure what to say. But as I looked at Joanna, I knew that she would wait all day if she had to.

'How about the supermarket first?' I said eventually.

Without a word, she got up and we left. Slowly I'm learning to choose what to do or eat and decide if I'm hungry or thirsty. But there's no escape from decision-making when it comes to our wedding in June, which is only a couple of months away.

Joanna is so busy at work that I'm doing a lot of the organising. She dreamed of this day for so long that she collected more than a hundred gold plates that she wanted to use for our guests. But when we realised that so many people would have to come from far away we decided to do something very different and we're going to have a simple service in a church attended by just eight people – my parents, David and Kim, Joanna's mother and three of her friends who live in England. However small our wedding is going to be, food, flowers, outfits, transportation, venues and menus must still be arranged. There are so many details, in fact, that I've built a file full of information that

Joanna and I read through together before deciding what we want.

The only aspect that I'm completely certain of is the ring I had made for Joanna before I left South Africa. It is a wide band made of yellow gold, which is dotted with diamonds and filigree work bearing the symbol of two mussel shells nestling together. They represent our love because nothing can prize mussels apart once they fuse together as one on a beach – even the might of the sea.

64

Waiting

The church is cool and quiet. At the end of long aisle stretching ahead of me, my mother, brother and sister sit in a pew; friends are in another. I'm waiting just inside the door of the church and gaze up at the huge stained-glass window behind the altar ahead of me. I'm glad that its colours are beginning to brighten. It rained a little earlier this morning and I don't want anything to ruin this day. But now I can see bright sunshine as I turn my head to look out of the door. It's the kind of glorious June day that seems to exist only in England with hedgerows thick with flowers, roses in bloom and an azure sky that appears endless overhead.

I think of Joanna. I've not seen her since early this morning before she left to get ready at the country house where we'll all go later to celebrate. It's a Georgian manor with lawns stretching green in front of it and lavender in beds around which bees fly lazily – picture perfect. None of us will forget this day. My mother smiles as I look down the aisle. She

has been glowing with happiness ever since she arrived from
South Africa. My brother and sister sit quietly beside her.
How good it is to see them here. My father is standing with me
because he is going to be my best man.

'She'll be here soon,' he says with a chuckle as he looks at
me. 'Don't get too worried.'

I won't. All I feel is a happy impatience to see Joanna. I'm
so anxious to marry her that I arrived nearly two hours ago.
I'm glad Dad is beside me as I wait. As he helped me get
dressed earlier – buttoning up my white shirt and tying my red
cravat, helping me into my charcoal-grey pin-striped suit and
lacing up my black shoes – I realised that his quiet and steady
presence was what I needed most today of all days. It gives
me such a familiar feeling of reassurance; it's one of the earliest memories I have, after all.

I wonder now if Dad is thinking about his own wedding
day as quiet contentment radiates from him. My parents' married life has been far from easy and I suspect that neither of
them can believe this day has arrived. They remind me of
children who dare not think a fairy tale is coming true at last.
Their eyes have been a little brighter, their smiles wider as
Joanna and I have shown them our flat and all the other details
of our life here. They have celebrated each one with us.

It is 1.25 p.m. Joanna will now be in the horse-drawn carriage that is bringing her to the church. She will look like a
fairy-tale princess and I am her less than traditional prince. I
think of her. Is she happy? Nervous? Only a few more minutes until I see her. I look down at the speech box that is sitting
on my knee. It's an old device I've had for a few years now,
a more sophisticated version of the black box my parents once

so nearly bought me. I don't often use it but I have it with me today because I must say my wedding vows to make them legal. Apparently, a person has to speak their promises for them to be binding and a witness must watch over me to vouch that I press the 'I will' button without being coerced into doing it.

Now I think of the words that I will soon say. Each was seared onto my memory one by one as I inputted them on my communication device.

> For better, for worse,
> For richer, for poorer,
> In sickness and in health,
> Til death do us part.

I'll never say words that mean more. Each syllable, each line, will reverberate inside me as I think of the vows I'm sealing with them. Is it possible that one month shy of the eight years since I was first assessed, I am sitting here about to commit my life to Joanna?

It is she who has taught me to understand the true meaning of the Bible passage we are having read during the service: 'There are three things that will endure – faith, hope and love – and the greatest of these is love.' My life has encompassed all three and I know the greatest of all is indeed love – in all its forms. I've experienced it as a boy and man, as a son, brother, grandson and friend, I've seen it between others and I know it can sustain us through the darkest of times. Now it's lifting me closer to the sun than I ever thought I would fly.

I hear a flurry of steps.

'She's here!' a voice cries. 'Close the doors!'

My father leans towards me as the organist starts to play.

'Are you ready, boy?' he asks.

I nod and he starts pushing me down the aisle as memories flash through my mind. I've seen so much. I've come so far. As I stop in front of the altar, there is a rustle of excitement and I turn my head to see Joanna. She is wearing a long white dress encrusted with crystals and a veil covers her face. She is holding a bouquet of red roses and she smiles. My heart stills.

I will not look back today. It is time to forget the past.

All I can think of is the future.

She is here.

She is walking towards me.

Joanna (Joan) and Martin just married – June 2009
© JeffTurnbull.com

Acknowledgements

I would like to thank my family, who have in no small way helped me to become the person I am today. Mum, Dad, Kim and David taught me many lessons – not least to laugh, the importance of family and sticking by each other through good times and bad. I love you all dearly.

Thank you to Pookie and Kojak for their unconditional love, which proved that dogs truly are man's best friend.

I would also like to thank Virna van der Walt, Erica Mbangamoh, Karin Faurie, Dr Kitty Uys, Professor Juan Bornman, Maureen Casey, Kerstin Tonsing, Dr Michal Harty, Simon Sikhosana, Dr Shakila Dada, Jéanette Loots, Corneli Strydom, Alecia Samuels, Professor Diane Nelson Bryen, Elaine Olivier, Sue Swenson, Cornè Kruger, Jackie Barker, Riëtte Pretorius, Ronell Alberts, Tricia Horne and Sandra Hartley for all their support and the lessons they taught me about the value of friendship.

There are so many others I would like to mention. Suffice to say I am indebted to friends, colleagues and complete strangers who have all in some way made a difference to my life and helped me on my journey through it.

To all my friends and colleagues at the Centre for Augmentative and Alternative Communication, thanks for your help, support and the years we spent together. I would also like to thank God, without whom I wouldn't be here today and for all the blessings I have and continue to receive.

Thank you also to Cilliers du Preez, who was always willing to help me with computer problems, to Albie Bester at Microsoft South Africa and Paul and Barney Hawes and the rest of the folk at Sensory Software, who were always there to lend a hand when it was needed.

Finally, thank you to Ivan Mulcahy, who was never more than an email away, Kerri Sharp at Simon & Schuster, who believed in my story, and last but not least Megan Lloyd Davies for the hours of hard work and the journey that was the writing of this book.

You can find out more about Martin and augmentative and alternative communication (AAC) on his personal website www.martinpistorius.com.